IN SEARCH
OF
Angels

IN SEARCH
OF
Angels

A Celestial Sourcebook
for Beginning Your Journey

David Connolly

A PERIGEE BOOK

Perigee Books
are published by
The Putnam Publishing Group
200 Madison Avenue
New York, NY 10016

Library of Congress Cataloging-in-Publication Data

Connolly, David, date.
In search of angels : a celestial sourcebook for beginning your
journey / David Connolly.
p.   cm.
Includes bibliographical references.
ISBN 0-399-51851-7 (alk. paper)
1. Angels. 2. Spiritual life. I. Title.
BL477.C65   1994
291.2′15—dc20   93-26752 CIP

Book design by Rhea Braunstein

Cover design by Isabella Fasciano
Cover lithograph, "Israfel," by Hugo Steiner-Prag

Printed in the United States of America
1   2   3   4   5   6   7   8   9   10

This book is printed on acid-free paper.
∞

Acknowledgments

I greatly appreciate the thoughtful attention and nourishing support given to me and this book during its creation. The eminent publisher Jeremy Tarcher is ANGELS' noble and self-appointed godfather, and he was its principal cheerleader for several otherwise lonesome months. I was heartened many times by his encouraging words.

My editor, Laura Shepherd, displayed great tact and literary skill, and a terrific attitude, and she made my experience as a rookie author a smooth and enjoyable one. Her ever-upbeat work-mate, Lisa Swayne, was a whiz and a wonder.

Several friends were especially helpful and supportive. Big thanks to Jeffrey Beth, Dorit Ilani, Suzy Hertzberg Liptrap, and Lyndon Stambler.

Special thanks also to Marilynn Webber, Mordecai Finley, Jane Howard, and many others for sharing their stories.

Contents

INTRODUCTION 9

1 Real or ethereal?
  What are angels? 13

2 On a wing and a prayer
  Agents of the sacred service 27

3 Amazing grace
  Exploring the angelic nature 55

4 Pigeonholing the "birds of God"
  Counting and categorizing the heavenly host 75

5 Feathers and light
  The appearance of angels and their images in art 101

6 The spirits of our times
  Contemporary beliefs and stories of angels 123

GLOSSARY OF ANGELIC TERMS 149

BIBLIOGRAPHY 152

LIST OF ILLUSTRATIONS 156

Introduction

*"May I burst with jubilant praise to assenting
angels."*
—Rainer Maria Rilke

he idea of writing a book about angels didn't come to me in a sudden flash of inspiration but over a period of several years. It started when I designed and constructed three-dimensional figures of angels made from paper as holiday gifts for my friends. After the holiday season had passed, I noticed that many of the angels were not put away with the other decorations, but ended up as year-round household adornments. This was my first conscious realization of the degree to which angels are a deeply rooted idea and symbol in everyday life.

Suddenly I was noticing angels everywhere, and I became aware of references and allusions to them in conversation, books, songs, movies, and advertising. Representations of angels in art and their different manifestations drew my attention and interest. I realized angels were common symbols of beauty, grace, wisdom, strength, mercy, peace, innocence, truth, hope, and guardianship.

With no particular end in mind, I went to libraries and found discussions of angels from many points of view throughout the historical past—theological, artistic, literary, philosophical, metaphysical, and psychological. I took notes for my own amusement and diversion and collected them in a folder that eventually was bursting with odd bits of scribbled paper.

Then I became interested in knowing what people think about angels today. So I worked up a simple questionnaire, and sent it to a network of friends. Many of their responses acted as the inspiration for this book.

Carl Jung once wrote: "The angel personifies the coming into consciousness of something new arising from the deep unconscious." Somewhere along the line I became mindful of my own aspiration to write about angels, and I sat down at my computer and began typing away.

In Search of Angels is a threshold into some of the extraordinary ideas and images of angels from the past and present. I've compiled this information from many historical sources, and from my questionnaire and personal interviews, which probe current attitudes, beliefs, and experiences. Rather than a forum for my own opinions, this book is much more an organized collection of interesting thoughts and insights of renowned people of the past and everyday people of the present. And rather than trying to arrive at emphatic conclusions and judgments, I welcome each reader to evolve his or her own impressions, conceptions, and questions about this universally endearing subject.

The chapters are organized to discuss a few basic questions and topics:

- What are angels?
- What are their roles and functions?

- What are angels like; what is their nature?
- How many angels are there; how are they organized; what are their names?
- The appearance of angels and their images in art.
- Contemporary beliefs and experiences.

The book is interspersed with illuminating quotes from such diverse personalities as William Shakespeare, Abraham Lincoln, John Locke, Emanuel Swedenborg, John Milton, Voltaire, Ralph Waldo Emerson, Edna St. Vincent Millay, John Donne, Edgar Allan Poe, Mary Baker Eddy, and Saints Ambrose, Augustine, Ephrem, Joan of Arc, Patrick, Paul, and Thomas Aquinas, among others, as well as from traditional religious works.

There is a verse from the New Testament letter to the Hebrews that says, "Do not neglect to show hospitality to strangers, for thereby some have entertained angels unawares." I think that these "strangers" can include the unfamiliar thoughts and speculations of people throughout the ages who have wondered at and rejoiced in the angels. Let the words of the many persons who contributed to this book reach into your heart and mind. And though, perhaps, at first you might entertain angels "unawares," you may find that—a little bit at a time, and in your own unique way—you will begin to see the invisible, feel the impalpable, hear the silence, and comprehend the unknowable.

1 Real or ethereal? What are angels?

"Every breath of air and ray of light and heat, every beautiful prospect, is, as it were, the skirt of their garments, the waving of the robes of those whose faces see God."
—*John Henry Newman*

ngel" is a common word in our language. There's spongy-soft angel food cake and delicate angel hair pasta. Elegant angel fish grace the aquaria of fish lovers. The longest uninterrupted waterfall in the world is Angel Falls, in Venezuela. The largest city in western North America is named simply "The Angels."

A singer with unusual purity of tone has "the voice of an angel." A child, when sleeping sweetly, "looks like an angel." Someone coming to our aid in a time of acute need is an "angel of mercy." It's an often-used, contemporary word for an extraordinary and ancient idea: an angel.

FROM THE BEGINNING

According to Genesis, angels have been a part of human history since the time of Adam and Eve, when, "at the east of the Garden of Eden," God placed "the cherubim, and a flaming sword which turned every way, to guard the way to the tree of life." And in *Paradise Lost,* the great epic poem by the English Puritan poet John Milton, angels guarded Paradise and were friendly companions and teachers to the first man and woman.

The particular western notion of benevolent spirit beings that most people today would quickly identify as angels developed from Judeo-Christian and Islamic lore, which were in turn influenced by earlier Persian, Greek, Babylonian, Chaldean, and Sumerian beliefs, among others. For more than 3,000 years, angels have been a persistent idea and image, an archetype and icon, in the collective awareness of western culture. They've figured prominently in secular folktales and traditional religious drama. Prophets dreamed of angels, mystics saw them, saints spoke with them, and the suffering prayed to them.

Visions of angels inspired great artists, from Leonardo and Michelangelo to Rubens and Rembrandt to Gauguin and Chagall, to create their images. Poets Dante, Milton, Goethe, Blake, Longfellow, Tennyson, Poe, Dickinson, Rilke, and others felt compelled to write of them. From Socrates to Nietzsche, learned philosophers opined about angels and their nature. And in a *Syntopicon* of the 102 most significant subjects of western thought, the editors of the *Encyclopaedia Britannica* selected as their first entry the subject "Angel."

BELIEF IN ANGELS

More than half of the people living in the United States today believe in the existence of angels. So do hundreds of millions of others around the world. For some, belief in angels reflects their assurance that the scriptures of their religion are the revelatory word of God. The sacred books of

the three major monotheistic faiths of the east and west—
Judaism, Christianity, and Islam—contain many references
to angels in heaven and on earth. So, for the religiously inclined, the frequent mention of angels in the Bible, the Koran, and other orthodox writings is sufficient proof of the
angels' existence.

> *"I believe in angels because the Bible says there are*
> *angels; and I believe the Bible to be the true*
> *Word of God."*
> *—Billy Graham*

For others, belief in angels comes as a "scientific" obser-
vation deduced from the natural order of the plant and animal species. Many great philosophers explained the
existence of angels using what is called the Chain of Being
Theory. The argument goes like this:

There is an uninterrupted chain in nature of increasing
biological complexity and intellectual capacity. In the natural life of the earth, this chain begins at the bottom with
the simplest plant organisms and works its way up through
all the plant and animal species to human beings. The differences between the successive "links"—or lifeforms—in
the chain are relatively small.

Because the difference between the nature of humans
and God seems so great, there must necessarily be intelligent beings forming the link, or links, in the chain between
humans and God. Just as humans look "down" the chain
at the animal and plant species, we should also be able to
look "up" at the higher beings we call angels.

> *"When we consider the infinite power and wisdom of the*
> *Maker, we have reason to think that it is suitable to the*
> *magnificent harmony of the universe, and the great*

design and infinite goodness of the architect, that the species of creature should also, by gentle degrees, ascend upwards from us toward his infinite perfection, as we see them gradually descend from us downward."

—*John Locke*

To put it simply, this argument says that angels exist because, as St. Thomas Aquinas, the eminent medieval scholar and theologian, concluded, "the universe would be incomplete without them."

Just as angels fill an apparent gap in the physical universe, they can also occupy an important psychological void in the human inner universe. As benign intelligences positioned biologically, intellectually, and spiritually between ourselves and God, angels are a graspable intermediary between humans and the mysterious power thought to be the source of all life, energy, and order in creation.

For many other people, tenets of religious faith and scientific or philosophical arguments that testify to the existence of angels are unnecessary. For them the reality of angels is self-evident. They believe they directly see or sense the presence and influence of angels in their lives—some occasionally, some daily, others constantly. Though many people over many centuries have written of their personal experiences with angels, the vast majority who feel touched by them have not. But their interactions with angels are no less meaningful than for those inclined to share their experience.

THE STUDY OF ANGELS

Accounts of angels described by historical figures, even centuries apart, can have striking similarities. Others have considerable differences. These inconsistencies naturally beg the question: just what are angels really?

Many people are content to believe what they believe about angels; they are satisfied with the extent of their understanding and feel no curiosity or need to expand it. But others suspect that this question might open a new door of learning and meaning that will enrich them and expand their daily experience of life. After all, you needn't have a conscious, committed belief in angels to enjoy and be inspired by them. For many centuries there have been thinkers, wonderers, dreamers, and arguers about angels. There is even a scholarly-sounding name for the study of angels: angelology.

If you picked this book up out of curiosity, you are probably disposed to an interest in angels. Even if you do not consider yourself the scholarly type, you may regard yourself a budding angelologist and the questing companion of the many men and women who have gone before you in this delightful endeavor.

TOWARD A DEFINITION

The word "angel" comes from the Greek word "angelos," which is itself the translation of the Hebrew word "malakh," meaning "messenger." Somehow, though, naming angels through a job description seems inadequate, even unworthy, of them.

> *"The name Angel refers to their office, not their nature.*
> *You ask the name of this nature, it is spirit; you*
> *ask its office, it is that of an Angel, which*
> *is a messenger."*
> —*St. Augustine*

Though angels in folktales and traditional religious stories often act as messengers from God to humans, they reportedly fill many different roles and functions, including guardians, guides, musicians, teachers, healers, comforters, and warriors, to name a few. Other Hebrew and Aramaic words for angels, although used less frequently in the Bible and elsewhere, translate into English as "the mighty," "sons of God," "ministers," "servants," "holy ones," and "watchers."

The first-century Jewish philosopher Philo of Alexandria said that God shows himself to humans as an angel, but each person experiences that divine expression differently. This book, then, is really the beginning of an exploration of an experience that will never be the same for any two people. That is part of the inherent beauty of the quest. We can, however, start with some common beliefs and use them as a basis for building a greater personal understanding.

The *New Catholic Encyclopedia* offers a definition of angels that is short but pithy: "Celestial spirits who serve God in various capacities." "Celestial" means heavenly or divine. "Spirits" are non-physical beings or intelligences. To "serve God" is given as the reason for the angels' existence, and the phrase "in various capacities" generically allows for all of the activities and functions traditionally attributed to angels.

Let's look more closely at each of these ideas.

CELESTIAL INHABITANTS

"I saw the Lord sitting on his throne, and all the host of heaven standing beside him on his right hand and his left."
—*1 Kings 22:19*

The first verse of the Old Testament book of Genesis provides, for some angel scholars, a basis for understanding the celestial origin and nature of angels. "In the beginning God created the heavens and earth" is explained to show that there are two distinct aspects of existence—"the heavens" and "earth." Earth, in this interpretation, represents the physical universe, and the heavens represent all of creation which transcends the boundaries of time, space, and matter.

Because our perception and intelligence basically operate within physical limitations, our thinking and imagination are confined, to a great degree, to those parameters. A clear understanding of "the heavens" as a "place" is a challenging concept. Cognizant of this uncertainty, the eighteenth-century French author and philosopher Voltaire wrote, with a hint of distress, "It is not known precisely where angels dwell—whether in the air, in the void, or the planets. It has not been God's pleasure that we should be informed of their abode."

Some scholars have speculated that the home of the angels is not so much a place as a state of being that coexists with and interpenetrates the physical universe. On this point the seventeenth-century German mystic Jakob Böhme said, "The holy angels converse and walk up and down in the innermost of the world."

But in whatever reality the angels live, it is fundamentally different from our own and seems wondrous to us. There are few things as stimulating to the human mind as speculation about extra-terrestrial intelligence. Because angels are celestial entities, the indigenous inhabitants of heaven, they are even more remarkable and mysterious to our imagination. For what must life be like in the environment that God reportedly calls home?

We attribute to angels a character and qualities that express their proximity to God. They are divine, they are pure, they are powerful, they are beautiful, they are holy. And because angels are literally "out of this world," they come to earth in the service of God with a perspective and agenda presumably more universal than our own.

SPIRIT BEINGS

> *"They are celestial visitants, flying on spiritual, not material, pinions. Angels are pure thoughts of God, winged with Truth and Love, no matter what their individualism may be."*
> —Mary Baker Eddy

So far we've discussed angels without encountering controversy or discord, but there are many ideas in the study of angels that spark varied opinions. The topic of the spirituality of angels has historically been a point of contention.

From what we've learned so far, the issue of spirituality might appear to be black and white. As mentioned above, the earth is physical, substantial; and the creatures of the earth have physical bodies, without which they cannot exist as earth lifeforms. The heavens are non-physical, purely spiritual, and since the angels are heavenly beings they must be entirely spiritual and non-material. Right?

ANGELS APPEAR TO HUMANS

> *"Angels, who are God's messengers, turn themselves into different shapes."*
> —From the Zohar, the "Book of Splendor" of the Cabala

Despite their supposedly purely spiritual, non-material nature, angels appear to people and interact with them in many accounts of scripture and popular lore. Abraham, Jacob, Lot, Moses, Daniel, Balaam, Gideon, Joshua, Eli-

jah, David, and others in stories of the Old Testament actually saw angels. In the Christian gospels, angels visited
and spoke to John the Baptist's father, Zechariah; the Virgin Mary; her spouse, Joseph; the shepherds around Bethlehem at the time of the birth of Jesus; Jesus himself in the
garden of Gethsemane; and the women who came to Jesus'
tomb to recover his body.

In Islamic legend the archangel Gabriel (Jibril in Arabic) appeared to Muhammad, commanded him to dictate the Koran, and guided him through the seven Moslem heavens.

St. Patrick's seventh-century biographer, Muirchu, wrote that the angel Victor (Victorius in Latin) visited St. Patrick "on every seventh day of the week; and as one man to another, so Patrick enjoyed conversation."

Joan of Arc, the fifteenth-century French heroine of Orléans, said she saw angels several times a week and that the Archangel Michael encouraged her to rise up and lead the fight for the king of France against the English. St. Joan is said to have exclaimed, "I saw them with my bodily eyes as clearly as I see you. And when they departed, I used to weep and wish that they would take me with them."

As a boy, the eighteenth-century English poet, painter, and engraver William Blake saw "a tree filled with angels; bright angelic wings bespangled every bough like stars."

The nineteenth-century French curé Père Lamy reported that he regularly saw angels and conversed with them.

Even today many people report experiences of seeing angels.

A PARADOXICAL CONFLICT?

If angels are entirely spiritual beings, how can they be seen on earth by people? How can they talk to us and interact with us in the manner in which they've been reported? As mentioned, there are different opinions.

Two of the most dominant source texts on the subject of angels were the sixth-century writings *The Celestial Hierarchy* and *Mystical Theology*, which, for many centuries, were the definitive word in Christian scholarship on the organizational structure of heaven. The teachings found in these works first took hold in the eastern church and later in the west, after they were translated from Greek to Latin in the ninth century.

The authorship of these books was imputed to the first-century bishop of Athens, Dionysius the Areopagite, who was reputed to be a personal convert and associate of St. Paul's. The actual writer(s) of these books has never been determined. This confusion gave a glow of authenticity to the works of Dionysius—sometimes called the Pseudo-Areopagite, or Pseudo-Dionysius—that they might otherwise not have had. In time, the Areopagite's belief in angels as entirely spiritual beings predominated within the Roman Catholic Church and secular culture at large.

But prior to Dionysius, scholars often guessed that angels were composed of elements less dense than humans. St. Paul, for example, in I Corinthians of the New Testament, states, "For not all flesh is alike . . . There are celestial bodies and there are terrestrial bodies . . ." The second-century Christian theologian Justin speculated that angels have ethereal bodies. The noted fourth-century writer Lactantius called angels the "breaths of God" and also thought them made of some fine ethereal matter. John Cassian, a monk writing in the fifth century, said, "For though we maintain that some spiritual natures exist, such as angels, archangels and other powers . . . yet we ought certainly not to consider them incorporeal. For they have in their own fashion a body in which they exist . . ." St. Fulgentius, a sixth-century bishop of Ecija, Spain, believed that angels have bodies of fire. This is also written in the Jewish Talmud and Cabala, and in the Islamic Koran.

The thirteenth-century scholastic giant St. Thomas Aquinas was an ardent affirmer of the writings of Dionysius. He stated emphatically in several of his books that angels are pure intellect, but can assume bodies at will.

Mortimer Adler, the noted twentieth-century American thinker, wrote that angels accomplish this "with bodies that they take on as guises but do not inhabit." He explains that "the bodies they appear to have are not really bodies or indispensable to their life . . . their corporeal forms are merely 'assumed bodies' . . . taken on by angels as guises only for the sake of engaging in their earthly ministry . . . When angels return to their heavenly home . . . [they] must discard every vestige of corporeality."

But in the centuries between Thomas Aquinas and Mr. Adler, many contradictory opinions emerged. For Thomas Hobbes, the seventeenth-century materialist philosopher, the existence of anything non-material was impossible. He believed biblical reports of angels seen by humans were "supernatural apparitions of the fancy, raised by the special and extraordinary operation of God." Hobbes thought that God created these deliberate apparitions "to make His presence and commandments known to mankind."

Emanuel Swedenborg, the eighteenth-century Swedish scientist, mystic, and theologian, whose teachings are followed by members of the New Jerusalem Church, believed strongly in the physical bodies of angels. In several books, Swedenborg wrote of his three decades of experiences with angels. "I have seen a thousand times," he said, "that angels are human form, or men, for I have conversed with them as man to man, sometimes with one alone, sometimes with many in company." In his descriptions of heaven, Swedenborg sketches a very earth-like, material lifestyle; his angels wear colorful clothing, marry one another, have houses and gardens "and other things familiar to those which exist on earth, but, of course, infinitely more beautiful and perfect."

The Scottish theologian John Duns Scotus, a contemporary and scholastic rival of Thomas Aquinas, believed that angels are composed of "spiritual matter"—a substance incorporeal and immaterial to human perception, but of some density when compared with the perfect spirituality of God.

"Spiritual matter," at least as a phrase, sounds like an oxymoron, but in angelic affairs it helps to keep in mind the caution offered by Joseph Glanvill, the seventeenth-century English writer and cleric: "What's impossible to all humanity may be possible to the metaphysics and physiology of angels."

UNSEEN BUT NOT UNNOTICED

Arguments for and against the way angels physically appear to humans are fascinating and prod us to comprehend their nature. For the most part, though, the activities of angels are thought to go on unseen, but not unnoticed. By far, most of the people questioned and interviewed for this book who reported that angels had communicated with them, or acted for them in their lives, did not see angels or hear them speak out loud. Rather, these men and women stated that their perception of the presence of angels was experienced chiefly on the level of their feelings or intuition, or in the heightened sense of awareness many people have during circumstances of extraordinary "coincidence," or "synchronicity."

> *"Make yourself familiar with angels, and behold them*
> *frequently in spirit; for, without being seen, they are*
> *present with you."*
> —St. Francis de Sales

IN THE SERVICE OF GOD
"Are they not all ministering servants sent forth to serve?"
—Hebrews 1:14

There is universal agreement that the angels' purpose is to act in the service of God—either in heaven, on earth, or as the intermediaries between the two. Even the Christian Protestant reformers concurred, despite their tendency to focus attention on the Word of God solely as it is given in Christian scripture, therefore downplaying the existence of angels and their role in spiritual life. Martin Luther himself, the first Protestant, said that angels act as "the Lord's soldiers, guardians, leaders, and protectors to preserve the creatures which He had created." Luther grumblingly conceded that "God rules the world through the agency of his holy angels," but then added, "Just why God thus exerts his rule, Scripture does not tell us."

The angels themselves confirm their status as the servants and agents of God. Speaking to Muhammad in the Koran, the Archangel Gabriel tells him, "We do not descend from heaven save at the bidding of your Lord." And the Archangel Raphael tells Adam in Milton's *Paradise Lost*, "Myself, and all th' Angelic Host, that stand/In the sight of God enthroned, our happy state/Hold, as you yours, while our obedience holds./On other surety none: freely we serve,/Because we freely love . . ."

In freely choosing to serve as the agents of divine purpose, angels are the living expression of the prayer "Thy will be done." And because of their attunement to God and the fulfillment of God's desires, we associate angels with many divine attributes that help them accomplish their office—love, faith, truth, hope, wisdom, strength, and understanding among them.

Angels apply themselves to many different kinds of activities under the general heading of "serving God," which we will discuss in the next chapter.

2 On a wing and a prayer
Agents of the sacred service

*"For an angel of peace, a faithful guide, a guardian
of our souls and bodies, let us entreat the Lord."
—From a litany of the
Eastern Orthodox Church*

ccording to Genesis, "In the beginning, God created the heavens and the earth," the two aspects of creation. In their mission of service toward the unfoldment and evolution of the divine purpose, the angels reportedly execute many tasks in both the heavenly and earthly arenas. They also act as intermediary powers and intelligences between heaven and earth. In some capacities, angels function only in heaven. In others, angels help regulate the order and growth of the physical universe. Sometimes angels serve directly in aid to humans on earth. And sometimes angels span the gap of perception, communication, and understanding between what often seem the distant realities of heaven and earth, of God and humankind.

HEAVENLY ATTENDANTS OF GOD

*"All [the angels], as they circle in their orders, look/Aloft;
and downward, with such sway prevail,/That all with
mutual impulse tend to God."*
—Dante

Historically, scholars who discoursed on the hierarchical organization of the angels believed that only the "lowest" orders of angels are active in affairs outside of heaven. The majority of angels, they said—and all of those in the orders nearest to God—are exclusively absorbed in the sublime and blissful business of the spiritual realms.

*"Around the throne of God a band
Of glorious angels always stand."*
—Children's hymn

In his work the *Duino Elegies,* written between 1912 and 1922, the Austrian poet Rainer Maria Rilke uses the angel as a symbol of self-fulfillment or consciousness transcending the need for material existence. In the famous first line from the Second Elegy, Rilke writes, "Jeder Engel ist schrecklich": "Every angel is terrible." He explains this line by saying, "The Angel of the Elegies is the being who vouches for the recognition of a higher degree of reality in the invisible. Therefore, 'terrible' to us, because we . . . still depend on the visible."

The behavior of the angels who serve God is indicative of their nature as beings suffused with this "higher degree of reality"—a constant and direct awareness of the divine that needs no other external experience for fulfillment.

IN PRAISE OF GOD
> *"You shall see the angels circling around the Throne,*
> *giving glory to their Lord."*
> —*The Koran*

Traditionally, the angels' foremost activity is to glorify and praise God. The Jewish *Book of Enoch* says, "The first voice [of the angels] blessed the Lord of spirits for ever and for ever." And John, the author of the New Testament book of Revelation, wrote of his vision of heaven that "all the angels stood round the throne . . . and they fell on their faces before the throne and worshipped God, saying, 'Amen! Blessing and glory and wisdom and thanksgiving and honor and power and might be to our God for ever and ever! Amen!' "

> *"Praise him, all his angels,*
> *praise him, all his host."*
> —*Psalm 148:2*

For angels, this veneration is a self-regenerating cycle of devotion, in which the love of God is both the unending source and object of their attentions. In this role, Dante, the Italian epic poet of the early Renaissance, described the angels in heaven as an "army which beholds and sings the glory of the One who stirs its love."

ANGELS AS SINGERS AND MUSICIANS
> *" 'Holy, holy, holy' is what the angels sing . . ."*
> —*from a Christian hymn of the same name*

Angels are often described, or represented in art, as musicians praising and adoring God with songs and symphonies. They are popularly depicted in heaven as a chorus of singers or an orchestra of instrumental performers spontaneously offering hosannas—shouts and songs of glory—thankful hymns, and celestial recitals.

"Speak ye who best can tell, ye sons of light,
Angels, for ye behold him and with songs
And choral symphonies, day without night
Circling his throne rejoicing."
        —John Milton

Edgar Allan Poe wrote a poem about the Islamic angel of music whose voice is so dazzling it even affects the stars:

"In Heaven a spirit doth dwell
'Whose heart-strings are a lute;'

None sing so wildly well
As the angel Israfel.
And the giddy stars (so legends tell)
Ceasing their hymns, attend the spell
Of his voice, all mute . . ."

❁

Angels are mentioned in scripture as playing instruments—harps, cymbals, and trumpets—and are frequently portrayed as musicians in medieval and Renaissance art with viols, lutes, and flutes. The nineteenth-century American art historian Clara Erskine Waters wrote of these paintings: "There is much that appeals to our imagination in the thought of these heavenly musicians. We fancy their perfect instruments attuned to perfect voices, creating such harmonies as no earthly orchestra can reproduce."

> *"Ethereal minstrel! Pilgrim of the sky."*
> *—William Wordsworth*

THE COURTIERS OF HEAVEN
> *"[An angel] is a member of that family of wondrous*
> *beings who, ere the worlds were made, millions of ages*
> *back, have stood around the throne of God . . . and*
> *served him with a keen ecstatic love."*
> *—John Henry Newman*

Although heaven's angels as a group are particularly attentive to praising God, musically and otherwise, they are also said to engage in other important pursuits—namely, the administration of God's creation.

In Judeo-Christian belief, humans are created in the image of God, and life on earth reflects—to a lesser magnificence—life in heaven. And because kings ruled earthly kingdoms from their thrones, God was thought to be the model from which such rulership derived. God, therefore, must be like a king enthroned in heaven. "The Lord," we are told in Psalm 103, "has established his throne in the heavens, and his kingdom rules over all." The New Testament gospel of Matthew calls heaven "the throne of God," and Islamic belief envisions a Throne of God in the seventh Moslem heaven. And from this seat of authority God rules all life in heaven and earth through a hierarchy of celestial attendants.

Just as the royal courts of earth are filled with busy courtiers, the court of heaven is administered by a teeming host of angels occupied with the operation of the heavenly government. In his epic, *The Divine Comedy*, Dante likens the appearance of heaven to "a pure white rose," in which busy angels move:

> *"Even as a swarm of bees that penetrates*
> *Within the flower and thence makes swift return*
> *Whither their toil yields savorous reward,*
> *So it descended into that great flower adorned*
> *With leaves so plenteous, and coming forth*
> *Sped back to where its love forever dwells."*

❈

REGULATORS AND OVERSEERS OF NATURAL LAW

> *"Every visible thing in this world is put in charge of*
> *an angel."*
> —*St. Augustine*

In heaven, angels are engaged in their divine duties as praisers and thanksgivers, as choristers, and administrative courtiers. Though mostly unseen in the physical universe, angels have been historically thought to preside over the forces of nature and to guide all of natural life.

Christian scholar Clement of Alexandria of the second century, the eleventh-century Persian-Jewish philosopher Avicenna, and the seventeenth-century German astronomer Johannes Kepler all believed that angels propel the stars and thus coordinate the vast and intricate movement of the entire cosmos.

The third-century Christian theologian Origen wrote that angels are placed over the four elements—earth, water, air, and fire—and over plants and animals. The Jewish Talmud also gives angels dominion over the elements as well as the seasons, and the *Book of Enoch* sets angels over hail, wind, lightning, storm, comets, whirlwind, hurricane, thunder, earthquake, snow, rain, daylight, night, sun, moon, stars, and planets. The Islamic prophet Muhammad said that even every raindrop is accompanied by an angel.

According to Jewish tradition, and also to Origen, angels participate unseen at the events of conception and birth.

The great medieval Jewish scholar Moses Maimonides wrote, "For every force charged by God, may He be exalted, with some business is an angel put in charge of that thing." Thomas Aquinas believed that "material things are controlled by angels." Nineteenth-century Roman Catholic Cardinal John Henry Newman wrote that angels are "what are called the laws of nature." And the Moslem scholar Mirza Ghulam Ahmad said that "the All-Wise One has instituted two systems for the proper functioning of the universe. The invisible system is related to the angels and there is no branch of the visible system that has not behind it the invisible system ... whatever is happening in the physical system also does not take place without the mediation of angels. God Almighty has called angels regulators and distributors, and they are the cause of every change and development."

As a part of the angels' responsibility for "every visible thing in this world," they are said to directly serve each human being.

ANGELS IN SERVICE TO HUMANKIND

*"Millions of spiritual creatures walk the earth
Unseen, both when we wake, and when we sleep."
—Adam to Eve, in* Paradise Lost

Though humans no doubt appreciate the acts of the angels in their unending praise of God, in the governing of God's kingdom, and in the regulation of natural law in the physical universe, what endears the angels to us most is their personal involvement in each human life. In the twelfth-century Moses Maimonides wrote that angels "are consecrated and devoted to the service of the Father and Creator, whose wont is to employ them as ministers and helpers, to have charge and care of mortal man." "Angels," said John Calvin, the sixteenth-century French reformer, "are the dispensers and administrators of the Divine beneficence toward us . . . they regard our safety, undertake our defense, direct our ways, and exercise a constant solicitude that no evil befall us." Though Calvin's words have a certain coolly functional ring to them, the direct experiences and consequences of this "divine beneficence" are warmly intimate and deeply touching to the human personality.

*"Aerial spirits, by great Jove designed
To be on earth the guardians of mankind;
Invisible to mortal eyes they go,
And mark our actions, good or bad, below;*

Th' immortal spies with watchful care preside,
And thrice ten thousand round their charges glide,
They can reward with glory or with gold;
Such power divine permission bids them hold."
                                    —*Hesiod*

No man or woman, it is said, is so self-sufficient as to neither need nor appreciate the gift of angelic support, nor is anyone so base or fallen to be passed over in the angels' ministry to humankind.

In their role as celestial servants to humans on earth, angels act variously as guardians, guides, teachers, strength-givers and comforters, protectors of the righteous, punishers of the wicked, and more.

GUARDIAN ANGELS

"For he will give his angels charge of you to guard you
in all your ways."
                    —*Psalm 91:11*

Undoubtedly the role of the angel as personal guardian is the most popularly beloved perception of them in the collective human belief of the past and present. Human life is often mysterious and frightening, and there is sometimes a profound need in us for a belief in attentive caring and protection greater than what can come from ourselves alone—an inner security gently extended from a higher love and wisdom to sustain us through the fears and dangers of human experience.

"Oh sovereign angel,
Wide-winged stranger above a forgetful earth,
Care for me, care for me. Keep me unaware of danger

And not regretful
And not forgetful of my innocent birth."
         —*Edna St. Vincent Millay*

Philo of Alexandria and Origen thought that two angels, one good and one bad, watch over each person. Robert Burton, the seventeenth-century English clergyman and writer, agreed, saying, "Every man hath a good and bad angel attending on him in particular all his life long." Even today, children in religious school are sometimes taught that a good angel sits on their right shoulder and a devil on their left, and that they can listen to the whispered advice of either.

Since the time of Thomas Aquinas, though, it is more often believed that a single beneficent angel watches over each human being. Angelic guardianship, Thomas Aquinas wrote, begins at the moment of birth and continues without interruption for every moment of human life.

"For every soul, there is a guardian watching it."
         —*The Koran*

Current New Age beliefs espouse the idea that often several angels are set as spiritual guardians and guides over each living person. John Calvin, the Protestant reformer, believed that "not one angel only has the care of every one of us, but that all the angels together with one consent watch over our salvation."

Angels are also thought to watch over national and ethnic groups as a whole. According to Jewish tradition, each of the seventy nations of humankind is watched over collectively by an angel-prince.

ANGELS AS GUIDES

> *"O brethren, my way, my way's cloudy,*
> *Go send-a them angels down."*
> —*Traditional African-American Spiritual*

At times each human being faces the uncertainty of how to proceed with the direction of their life. Angels are said to be spiritual guides on our life's journey; they help to direct our hearts and minds to an understanding of God and ourselves, and to finding our way in the world.

> *"These upward-soaring beings never lead towards self,*
> *sin, or materiality, but guide to the divine principle of*
> *all good."*
> —*Mary Baker Eddy*

Fourteenth-century Dominican theologian and mystic Johannes "Meister" Eckhart wrote that angels help guide humans to a personal inner experience of God—saying that angels "abet and assist God's birth in the soul."

The Jewish Cabala says that angels guide human ability to acquire intellectual knowledge. On this point, Thomas Aquinas wrote that "human intellectual knowledge is ordered by God through the mediation of angels."

Thomas Aquinas also believed that angels guide humans to acts of choice. "A person," he wrote, "is disposed to an act of choice by an angel . . . in two ways. Sometimes, a man's understanding is enlightened by an angel to know what is good, but it is not instructed as to the reason why . . . But sometimes he is instructed by angelic illumination, both that this act is good and as to the reason why it is good . . ."

*"Behold, I send an angel before you, to guard you on
the way and to bring you to the place which I
have prepared. Give heed to him and hearken
to his voice . . ."*
—*Exodus 23:20–21*

In many traditional stories angels act as guides leading humans on difficult journeys. The *Book of Tobit* is a popular Jewish folktale, scenes from which were often painted by artists of the Middle Ages and Renaissance. In the story, the Archangel Raphael takes on the appearance of a man and guides and advises young Tobias on a long journey, in which Tobias recovers his family's wealth, meets and marries his wife, and generally lives happily ever after.

"The angel of God who went before the host of Israel" led the Hebrew people in their exodus from Egypt and, assuming the form of a pillar of cloud, stood guard between the fleeing Israelites and the pursuing Egyptians. The Archangel Gabriel was Muhammad's guide through the seven Islamic heavens. The Archangel Michael, in the appearance of a young deacon, is said to have safely guided St. Oringa after she became lost and endangered on her pilgrimage to the church at Mt. Gargano near Naples. In the Jewish tradition, an angel led the animals onto Noah's ark at the time of the Deluge.

*"There is an unseen hand, a guiding angel, that somehow,
like a submerged propeller, drives us on."*
—*Rabindranath Tagore*

ANGELS AS TEACHERS
*"The delight of the wisdom of the angels is to communicate
to others what they know."*
—*Emanuel Swedenborg*

Knowledge is a resource as precious to human life as breath, water, food, clothing, and shelter. Through knowledge, humans come to appreciate the wonder of the world around them and learn to prosper in it. Through knowledge comes an understanding of the self as an expression of the totality of life and the wisdom to exercise choices leading to meaningful experiences of it.

In guiding humans to the acquisition of knowledge and to an understanding and experience of God and the "good," angels act as unseen "inner" teachers. There are also many scriptural and popular accounts of angels as more literal, demonstrative teachers of humans.

Angels have often been associated with the origin and teaching of human languages. According to the Jewish *Testament of Naphtali,* seventy angels taught the seventy different nations of humankind their languages, and the Archangel Michael in particular taught Hebrew to the Jews.

Jewish folklore also maintains that Michael taught agriculture to Adam, and that angels taught Moses the arts of healing.

Twice in the Old Testament Daniel is instructed by the Archangel Gabriel, who tells him, "O Daniel, I have now come out to give you wisdom and understanding." An angel enlightened the Jewish prophet Zechariah regarding the meaning of a vision and answered his questions. In Milton's *Paradise Lost,* the Archangel Raphael tutored Adam on the war in heaven and answered his questions about the creation of the world and the motions of celestial bodies. In the *Book of Jubilees,* Gabriel explained to Moses about the time of creation and the events of Genesis, and angels imparted the knowledge of herbal medicine to Noah and the practice of law and justice to all of humankind.

In the Roman Catholic tradition, angels are said to have taught St. Anthony to make mats from palms, St. Ambrose to convert heretics, St. Savinian the meaning of the Psalms, and Veronica of Milan to read and sing. Angels are also said to have instructed builders on the proper locations and designs of many churches.

STRENGTH-GIVERS AND COMFORTERS
"Who, if I cried, would hear me among the angelic orders?"
—Rainer Maria Rilke

During difficult times when our own resources of endurance, hope, and rejuvenation feel depleted or altogether barren, angels are said to help restore and invigorate our being. In many traditional tales angels are nurturers, comforters, and strength-givers.

The Bible contains several stories in which angels give comfort and strength to humans. In the Old Testament book of I Kings, the prophet Elijah flees into the wilderness from the wrath of Jezebel, who has sworn to harm him. Elijah is tired and frightened and asks God "that he might die." As Elijah lies sleeping, an angel brings him "a cake baked on hot stones and a jar of water," wakes Elijah, and tells him to eat. Elijah eats the food and sleeps again, and the angel wakes Elijah a second time and orders him to eat more. "And he arose," the story says, "and ate and drank, and went in the strength of that food forty days and forty nights . . ."

In another story from the Old Testament the prophet Daniel fasted for three weeks and, while standing at the bank of the Tigris River, saw an angel. Describing his condition, Daniel says, "I was left alone and saw this great vision, and no strength was left in me; my radiant appearance was fearfully changed, and I retained no strength." Then, Daniel says, the angel "touched me and strengthened me . . . And when he spoke to me, I was strengthened . . ."

In the New Testament, angels gave strength and sustenance even to Jesus when he was alone in the desert for forty days and in his agony in the garden of Gethsemane.

"And there appeared to him an angel from heaven, strengthening him."
—Luke 22:43

In the book of Acts, an angel comforted St. Paul during a terrible storm at sea and reassured him that no one on board the ship would be harmed.

Within the legends of the Roman Catholic Church are stories of angels offering comfort and strength in times of great distress to many spiritual notables, including Saints Andeol, Concord, Euphemia, Lawrence, Sergius, Venantius, Vincent, George of Diospolis, Julian of Antioch, and Theodorus of Heraclea.

PROTECTORS AND RESCUERS OF THE RIGHTEOUS

"Angels and ministers of grace, defend us!"
—*Hamlet to Horatio in Shakespeare's* Hamlet

In the face of the moral confusion and apparent injustice prevalent in human life, it is heartening to hear that angels are said at times to actively intervene in the affairs of humankind on behalf of the innocent and righteous. The Bible tells many stories of the protective intercession of the angels, especially for the benefit of those faithful to God.

When God tested Abraham's faith by asking him to sacrifice his son, Isaac, an angel intervened to save the boy's life, telling Abraham as he was about to slay Isaac, "Do not lay your hand on the lad or do anything to him; for now I know that you fear God . . ."

The book of Daniel tells two stories of angels intervening to save the lives of faithful men. In the first, three Jewish

men—Shadrach, Meshach, and Abednego—are thrown into a roaring furnace for refusing to worship a golden idol created by the Babylonian king Nebuchadnezzar. But as the king watches, he sees four men walking about in the furnace, unharmed by the flames, "and the appearance of the fourth is like a son of the gods." So the king ordered them out of the furnace and "saw that the fire had not had any power over the bodies of those men . . . Nebuchadnez-zar said, 'Blessed be the God of Shadrach, Meshach, and Abednego, who has sent his angel and delivered his servants . . .' "

In the second tale, one of the most famous in all the Bi-ble, Daniel is thrown overnight into a den of lions as pun-ishment for petitioning God in prayer, after King Darius had decreed that no one in his kingdom should petition to any god or man but himself. At dawn, Darius goes to see what has happened to Daniel during the night, and Daniel tells him, "My God sent his angel and shut the lions' mouths, and they have not hurt me, because I was found blameless before him . . ."

> *"The angel of the Lord encamps around those who fear him, and delivers them."*
> —*Psalm* 34:7

In a story from Acts in the New Testament, St. Peter was imprisoned during Passover by order of King Herod, who planned to punish and perhaps kill Peter, as he had killed Peter's companion, James. During the night before Peter's trial, "an angel of the Lord appeared, and a light shone in the cell; and he struck Peter on the side and woke him, say-ing, 'Get up quickly.' And the chains fell off his hands. And the angel said to him, 'Dress yourself and put on your san-dals.' And he did so. And he said to him, 'Wrap your mantle around you and follow me.' " And the angel led Peter past the guards and out of the prison to freedom.

In the fifth century, St. Leo went out from Rome to meet with Attila the Hun, when the infamous barbarian was threatening to attack and pillage the city. Pope Leo implored Attila to spare the city and its inhabitants. To everyone's amazement, Attila immediately rounded up his army and departed the vicinity. When asked why, Attila is recorded to have explained, "While Pope Leo was speaking, I distinctly saw two shining beings of venerable aspect, and manifestly not of this earth, standing by his side. They had flaming swords in their hands, and menaced me with death if I refused to withdraw my army."

PUNISHERS AND DESTROYERS OF THE WICKED
    "Sovereign of heaven, send a good angel before us to
       spread terror and dismay."
       —II Maccabees 15:23

While they are typically caring and nurturing, angels also possess the capacity to act as ferocious warriors against that which displeases God.

Three different books of the Old Testament tell of the night when "the angel of the Lord slew a hundred and eighty-five thousand in the camp of the Assyrians," whose king, Sennacherib, mocked the Hebrew king Hezekiah and reviled the God of Israel.

Jewish legend also tells of angels who hurled arrows, great hailstones, and fire and brimstone at Pharaoh's forces during the Hebrews' flight from Egypt.

In the *Book of Tobit,* Tobias wishes to marry Sarah, whose seven previous husbands have been killed on their wedding nights by the demon Asmodeus. The Archangel Raphael tells Tobias how to chase away the demon by heating the heart and liver of a fish on burning incense. When Tobias does this, "the reek of the fish distressed the demon, who fled through the air to Egypt. Raphael pursued him there, shackled him, and strangled him forthwith."

Herod, the same arrogant king who took St. Peter prisoner, also met his end at the hand of "an angel of the Lord" who "smote him, because he did not give God the glory . . ."

In the New Testament book of Revelation, John describes how the Archangel Michael and his fellow angels fought and defeated Satan and his rebel forces in the War of Heaven. The seventeenth-century English poet John Milton recounts this event in *Paradise Lost* as a three-day battle, in which the Archangels Michael and Gabriel lead the "loyalist" host of heaven against Lucifer's army of dissident angels:

> *"Now storming fury rose,*
> *And clamor such as heard in Heaven till now*
> *Was never; arms on armour clashing brayed*
> *Horrible discord, and the madding wheels*
> *Of brazen chariots raged; dire was the noise*
> *Of conflict; overhead the dismal hiss*
> *Of fiery darts in flaming volleys flew,*
> *And, flying, vaulted either host with fire.*
> *So under fiery cope together rushed*
> *Both battles main, with ruinous assault*
> *And inextinguishable rage. All Heaven*
> *Resounded; and, had Earth been then, all Earth*
> *Had to her centre shook."*

ALL THIS AND MORE

"How oft do they their silver bowers leave
And come to succor us that succor want? . . .
They for us fight, they watch, and duly ward,
And their bright squadrons round about us plant,
And all for love, and nothing for reward!"
—*Edmund Spenser*

Guard, guide, comfort, teach, and protect us—all these things angels do and more. John Wesley, the eighteenth-century founder of Methodism, wrote that the angels serve humankind "in a thousand ways . . . They may assist us in our searching after truth, remove many doubts and difficulties . . . they may warn us of evil in disguise, and place what is good in a clear strong light. They may gently move our will to embrace what is good, and to fly from that which is evil."

A host of accounts—both scriptural and popular—remind us that human and angelic life are intimately interwoven.

The Koran says that "the heavens above well-nigh break apart as the angels . . . beg forgiveness for those on earth."

During the holiday season we feel the presence of the Angel of Peace.

The Archangel Raphael, after returning from his journey with Tobias, healed the blindness of Tobias' father, Tobit.

St. Hermann of Steinfeld reported seeing angels carrying incense among the members of the choir during Mass, and giving particularly joyous attention to those who sang fervently from the heart.

Saints Crispin and Crispinian were brothers and cobblers who made free shoes for the poor with the leather that was brought to them by angels.

There is a story about an angel who filled in as cook at a monastery when the regular chef was detained in the ecstatic reverie of his devotions.

St. Isidore (San Ysidro in Spanish), in his sixth-century youth, was a farm laborer who angered his fellow field-workers by going to Mass each morning. They complained to the farmer that Isidore wasted time and neglected his work. But when the farmer went to check on Isidore's industry, he saw three plows at work in the field, one guided by Isidore and two more guided by two angels, who helped him.

> *"So in a voice, so in a shapeless flame*
> *Angels affect us oft, and worshipped be."*
> —*John Donne*

ANGELS AS INTERMEDIARIES BETWEEN HEAVEN AND EARTH

> *"All arrangements that are carried out between heaven*
> *and earth are carried out through angels ..."*
> —*Mirza Ghulam Ahmad*

The monotheistic religions—Judaism, Christianity, and Islam—tend to think in polarities like good and evil, the saved and the damned, which consequently establishes spiritual distance between God and humans. So to many people in our culture, God can seem remote. Angels help to close that distance and make the will and care of God personal. The angels invite us to know God.

> *"The Angels stand between us and God, but they are*
> *translucent, even transparent, and they beckon us to*
> *penetrate their luminosity."*
> —*Peter Wilson*

The book of Genesis tells the story of how Jacob went to sleep on his journey from Beersheba to Haran: "And he dreamed that there was a ladder set up on the earth, and the top of it reached to heaven; and behold, the angels of God were ascending and descending on it!"

Jacob's dream of the ladder that bridges heaven and earth with angels coming and going symbolizes angels as intermediaries between God and humans. In their role as intermediaries angels act as messengers, recorders and reporters of human behavior, and conveyors of human souls to heaven at the time of death.

MESSENGERS FROM HEAVEN TO EARTH

"[God] sends forth the angels as His messengers, with two, three, or four pairs of wings."
—The Koran

As discussed in Chapter 1, the word "angel" comes from the Greek word for messenger. Angels are the messengers of God, and some of the grandest images of world legends come from accounts of angels appearing to humans in this capacity.

In Christian lore, angels brought messages at many significant times in the life of Jesus. Probably the most often portrayed scene of Renaissance painters is the Annunciation, in which the Archangel Gabriel, sent by God, appeared to the Virgin Mary in Nazareth to tell her, "Do not be afraid, Mary, for you have found favor with God. And behold, you will conceive in your womb and bear a son, and you shall call his name Jesus."

The birth of Jesus was announced by "an angel of the Lord," who appeared to the shepherds in the region of Bethlehem, saying, "Be not afraid; for behold, I bring you good news of a great joy which will come to all people; for to you is born this day in the city of David a savior, who is Christ the Lord. And this will be a sign for you: you will find a babe wrapped in swaddling clothes and lying in a manger." And when the angel finished his message, an entire chorus of musical angels is said to have sung to the people of earth.

> *"It came upon a midnight clear,*
> *That glorious song of old,*
> *From angels bending near the earth*
> *To touch their harps of gold.*
> *'Peace on the earth, good will to men*
> *From Heaven's all gracious King.'*
> *The world in solemn stillness lay*
> *To hear the angels sing."*
> *—Christmas hymn*

When Mary and Mary Magdalene came to Jesus' tomb to recover his body, they were met by an angel who told them, "Do not be afraid; for I know that you seek Jesus who was crucified. He is not here; for he is risen, as he said."

The Archangel Gabriel is also a special messenger in the Moslem tradition. Gabriel came to Muhammad one night during Ramadan, the month of fasting, and told him, "Recite! Recite in the name of your Lord who created— created man from clots of blood. Recite! Your Lord is the Most Bountiful One, who by the pen taught men what they did not know." And from this visitation and message, Muhammad began reciting the *suras* of the Koran.

In both the Moslem and Christian traditions, trumpeting angels will announce the end of the world and the Day of Judgment.

"At the round earth's imagin'd corners, blow
Your trumpets angels, and arise arise
From death, you numberless infinities
Of souls."
—*John Donne*

Angels are also said to carry messages from humans to
God—most popularly as the conveyers of prayers from
earth to heaven.

"They both convey the biddings of the Father to His
children and report the children's need to their Father."
—*Moses Maimonides*

RECORDERS AND REPORTERS OF THE DEEDS OF HUMANS
"There are two angels that attend unseen
Each one of us, and in great books record
Our good and evil deeds . . ."
—*Henry Wadsworth Longfellow*

The divine equity and karmic balance that exist beyond
the imperfect justice of earth connect each human with
unseen angels, who record and report on human acts to the
higher authority of heaven. According to *The Apocalypse of
St. Paul,* this accounting occurs daily "at the hour of morning which is the twelfth hour of the night" when "all the
angels of men and women go to meet God and present all
the work which every man has wrought, whether good or
evil."

"O, write my name, write my name,
The angels in heaven gonna write my name."
—*Traditional African-American spiritual*

CARRIERS OF SOULS TO HEAVEN
> *"I looked over Jordan and what did I see,*
> *Comin' for to carry me home?*
> *A band of angels, comin' after me,*
> *Comin' for to carry me home.*
> *Swing low, sweet chariot . . ."*
> —*Traditional African-American spiritual*

One of the most compassionate and moving of the reported acts of the angels is their conveying and accompanying the souls of humans to heaven at the time of death.

> *"He [God] sends forth guardians who watch over you*
> *and carry away your souls without fail when death*
> *overtakes you."*
> —*The Koran*

The changes and transitions that occur in the experience of the soul at the moment of its passing must be extraordinary and mysterious. To have the companionship and guidance of angels at such a time is a gift of great comfort and peace.

> *"Good night, sweet prince: and flights of angels sing*
> *thee to thy rest."*
> —*Horatio to a dying Hamlet in*
> *Shakespeare's* Hamlet

3 Amazing grace
Exploring the angelic nature

"Their Natures were clean and bright; they had clear, copious Displays of the divine Excellence, Perfection and Benignity round about them: Their internal, vivid, constant Sensation must assure them of the Joy and Bliss there is in the Favour and Enjoyment of that God, whom they served."
—John Reynolds

xternal behavior often mirrors the subjective, or more abstract, qualities of a being. By observing the activities of others, and the manner in which they carry out their duties and responsibilities in life, we infer values and characteristics of their inner nature. In Chapter 2 we looked at the roles and functions of the angels. And in learning what angels do, we also begin to grasp something of what they are. So through the variety and quality of the acts of the angels, we have already begun to learn about their nature.

As mentioned in the first chapter, angels are spiritual beings, who most often inhabit an immaterial realm of experience beyond our human capacity to fully perceive and know. It is paradoxical that our fascination with angels is rooted in their significant differences from ourselves, while at the same time it is difficult to comprehend them in any-

thing other than anthropomorphic terms. So when we consider what angels are like, we can really do no better than attribute to them a nature based on human experience and understanding.

> *"Human conjecture confers upon angels its own forms of thought . . . but this is only fancy. It has behind it no more reality than has the sculptor's thought when he carves his 'Statue of Liberty,' which embodies his conception of an unseen quality or condition."*
> —*Mary Baker Eddy*

If angels are a higher species of lifeform, as suggested by the Chain of Being Theory mentioned in Chapter 1, there may be many important aspects of their nature that we would never think to wonder about, because they are so foreign to our own familiar preoccupations. A pet dog, for example—primarily absorbed with food and rest and occasional playfulness and exercise—might consider humans as amazing creatures because of their seemingly exotic and extravagant behaviors in attending to eating, sleeping, and playing when compared to their own. But the dog does not seem to have the cerebral wherewithal to perceive or reflect on, for instance, common human intellectual and emotional experiences, or human creativity and communication. In the same way, there may be fundamental aspects of the angels' experience of life that are beyond the ability of the human imagination to ever consider.

> *"We cannot describe their condition in the terms of the conditions of men, the reality of whose attributes and the limits of whose qualities and whose movements and whose stillness we recognize and understand.*

*Allah has forbidden us that and has said: 'None knows
the hosts of thy Lord but He' " (Koran 74:32).*
—*Mirza Ghulam Ahmad*

Sometimes angel lovers have expressed an ironic regret that the very act of trying to take an "objective" inventory of the angels' special nature can diminish a holistic or poetical understanding of their true magic. On this point the English lyric poet of the nineteenth century John Keats wrote,

> *"Do not all charms fly*
> *At the mere touch of cold philosophy?*
> *There was an awful rainbow once in heaven:*
> *We know her woof, her texture; she is given*
> *In the dull catalogue of common things.*
> *Philosophy will clip an Angel's wings."*

❈

Even so, this has not deterred centuries of speculation about the nature of angels in scholarship and popular belief. And, not surprisingly, there have been a variety of opinions on many of these topics—about angels as intellectual beings, moral beings, immortal beings, and sexual beings, among others.

ANGELS AS INTELLECTUAL BEINGS

Historically, angelologists of a philosophical inclination showed a great curiosity about angels as intelligent beings and asked such questions as:

- Are the thought processes of angels similar to those of humans, or is their intellectual life different from our own?

- How do angels acquire knowledge? Do they ponder and judge the significance of external data before coming to an understanding, or do they come to some immediate, intuitive knowledge of a thing?
- Do angels struggle with mixed emotions and imperfect information to form often-tentative conclusions as humans do, or do they somehow come to a more perfect understanding?

The Jewish philosopher Philo called angels "incorporeal and happy souls . . . not mixtures of rational and irrational natures as ourselves are, but having the irrational nature cut out, wholly intelligent throughout . . ."

Writing in the thirteenth century, Thomas Aquinas said, "For the human intellect, although it can know itself, does indeed take the first beginning of its knowledge from without. . . . There is, therefore, a more perfect intellectual life in the angels. In them the intellect does not proceed to self-knowledge from anything exterior, but knows itself through itself." And Aquinas thought that the angels' knowledge is "incapable of defect," because "they see directly the pure truth about things by a simple intuition . . ."

The contemporary scholar Mortimer Adler believes that "the angelic mind is purely intellectual. It is nothing but an intellect . . . nothing but a power of understanding."

Adler agrees with Aquinas' idea about the inner-derived knowledge of the angels: "Unlike the human intellect, whose powers include that of judging and of reasoning, the angelic intellect does not think. It neither joins nor disjoins concepts to form judgments, as the human mind does; nor does it put judgments together in a process of reasoning that leads to a conclusion. In short, its action is neither cognitive nor discursive. It is purely intuitive."

And as to the source of this intuition, Adler says, "The

only conceivable answer is that the ideas involved in angelic knowledge and understanding must be innate or connatural ... Just as we, according to the Declaration of Independence, are endowed by our creator with certain unalienable rights, so the angels are endowed by their creator with certain infused ideas."

Adler again agrees with Aquinas that the angels' knowledge is superior to human knowledge, saying, "Angels are able to know and understand ... better than the human intellect can, precisely because such knowledge and understanding comes to them by way of ideas infused in them by God ..."

The extent of angelic knowledge is also thought to be superior to that of humans. In the Old Testament, the wise woman of Tekoa tells King David that he "has wisdom like the wisdom of the angel of God to know all things that are on the earth." A folk saying states that "nothing is hidden from the angels." St. Augustine wrote in the fifth century that the angels know everything of that "which is called the heaven; the gathering of the waters beneath, and the laying bare of the dry land, and the production of plants and trees; the creation of sun, moon, and stars; and of the animals out of the waters, fowls and fish, and monsters of the deep; and of everything that walks or creeps on the earth, and of man himself ..." John Wesley wrote that angels "no doubt clearly discern all our words and actions, if not all our thoughts too; for it is hard to think these walls of flesh and blood can intercept the view of an angelic being." And the *Zohar* of the Cabala teaches that angels know even men's futures.

But though the angels' knowledge of all things is considered extensive, they are not thought to be omniscient, as God is. As quoted by Mark in the New Testament, Jesus says to his disciples at the Mount of Olives in Jerusalem,

"But of that day or that hour no one knows, not even the angels in heaven . . . only the Father."

ANGELS AS MORAL BEINGS

Though some people have questioned the angels' capacity to think and act individually, independent from an unconsidered, robotic impulse to fulfill God's desires, most scholars have considered angels as beings gifted with the ability to distinguish right from wrong. More able, even, than humans, according to the wise woman from Tekoa, who complimented King David that he was "like the angel of God to discern good and evil."

Angels are also thought to have the free will to form personal, moral decisions and to choose actions in accordance with them. God, speaking of the angels in Milton's *Paradise Lost,* says that they are "authors to themselves in all/Both what they judge and what they choose; for so/I formed them free, and free they must remain." This distinction makes angels willing servants of God rather than automatons of God's moral domination.

In general, scholarly beliefs about the moral purity of the angels and their behavior have changed over time. Just as most early scholars speculated that angels were not entirely spiritual, as discussed in Chapter 1, they also thought that angels were less than pristine in thought and deed. With the ability to determine right and wrong, and with the freedom to choose their own actions, angels were not only thought theoretically capable of error, but actually errant at times. The Old Testament book of Job says of God that "his angels he charges with error." And the seventh-century Christian thinker John of Damascus wrote, "Though the angel is rational, intelligent, and possessing of free will, it is changeable, since all things are created mutable, and thus it has the potentiality either to improve or to turn toward evil."

Some early scholars, like Justin, believed that only some angels sinned. Others, like Origen, believed that all angels displeased God in some way.

Sometimes God forgave the angels for their mistakes. The New Testament writer Peter suggested that it was God's habit to "spare the angels when they sinned." But other stories tell of God punishing angels for their misdeeds. There is a Jewish tale of two angels who were expelled from heaven for one hundred thirty-eight years for prematurely disclosing God's decree of the destruction of Sodom and Gomorrah. And the New Testament book of Jude tells of "the angels that did not keep their own position but left their proper dwelling." As a consequence they "have been kept by him in eternal chains in the nether gloom until the judgment of the great day."

FALLEN ANGELS

Jewish, Christian, and Moslem tradition all have stories of "fallen" angels—angels who lost their place in heaven for acting against God's wishes.

Genesis, in the Old Testament, mentions the "sons of God," who came to earth because they saw that the "daughters of men were fair," took human wives, and "bore children to them." These offspring are described as "the mighty men that were of old, the men of renown." In Genesis, the angels are not criticized or punished for this behavior. But as the Jewish *Book of Enoch* interprets the same story, two hundred angels (called *nephillim*, the "Watchers"), acting without permission or direction of God, succumb to their lust for earth women and father monstrous and destructive offspring. Further, the Watchers teach humans about many things they're better off not knowing— weapons and warfare, enchantments, and secrets of heaven.

The giant children of the Watchers and their earthly

wives devour all the prepared food in the world, and then begin to eat birds, beasts, reptiles, fish, humans, and then one another. Finally God orders four angels—Michael, Gabriel, Raphael, and Uriel—to arrange for the giants to kill themselves off and to banish the Watchers to secret valleys of the earth until the day of judgment.

The Jewish *Book of Jubilees* and the Talmudic work *Midrash Arkir* also tell versions of the tale of the Watchers. In these two stories, the angels who descend to earth do so with pure intentions but are corrupted into sin after coming to earth. All of the tales of the Watchers attribute their downfall to succumbing to their lustful desires.

THE GREAT REBELLION

> *"Angels are bright still, though the brightest fell."*
> *—Malcolm to Macduff in Shakespeare's* Macbeth

Christian lore tells the story of how Satan, or Lucifer (whose name means "light-bearer"), once the greatest of the angels, led a rebellion in heaven against God and was defeated and deposed to hell. Versions of this story are given in Revelation in the New Testament and by the poets Dante and Milton. In the belief of the Catholic Church and other Christian sects, Satan is now a demonic spirit being who, with his army of the fallen angels, tempts and tricks humans into acts of sin against themselves, one another, and God.

> *"But oh, how fall'n! How changed*
> *From him who, in the happy realms of light,*
> *Clothed with transcendent brightness, didst outshine*
> *Myriads though bright!"*
> *—John Milton*

St. Augustine, writing about how the fall of the "bad" angels came about, said that "good and bad angels have arisen, not from a difference in their nature and origin . . . but from a difference in their wills and desires . . . While some steadfastly continued in that which was the common good of all, namely, in God Himself, and in His eternity, truth, and love; others . . . became proud, deceived, envious."

The Moslem tradition tells the story of how Allah, pleased at the creation of the first man, Adam, orders the angels to bow down in honor to Adam. But the foremost angel, Iblis, is overcome with pride and envy and refuses to bow down as Allah has commanded. And because of his prideful rejection of God's wishes, Iblis becomes an outcast from heaven.

ANGELS AS PERFECT BEINGS

Despite their early mistakes and transgressions in the eyes of God and humankind, over time, angels were seen more and more as morally perfect beings. In religious scripture and the popular vernacular, angels are called "holy," which the *American Encyclopedic Dictionary* defines as "consecrated, sacred; morally and spiritually perfect; belonging to, commissioned by, devoted to God; of high moral excellence . . ."

The early sixth-century writer Pseudo-Dionysius was the first influential angelologist to espouse the completely immaterial spirituality of angels. He also wrote that the angels live constantly in blessed communion with God and therefore willingly give themselves entirely to the pure good of God's nature. In the late sixth century, Pope Gregory the Great seconded this opinion and characterized angels as spotless, sinless, and happy beings. St. Thomas Aquinas wrote that for a short moment at the instant of their creation angels can choose between the will of God and other acts, and always and forever freely choose for God. The seventeenth-century English writer John Reynolds rhetorically asked, "Since these Sons of God were so pure within, and placed in such a perfect State and World, how could any Sin possibly possess their Minds or Wills?"

And so, over time, a belief in angels as morally perfect beings reflecting the divine nature of their creator came to predominate religious and popular thought.

ANGELIC VIRTUES AND ATTRIBUTES

In religious scripture, and in art throughout the ages, angels are shown as beings of celestial radiance. God calls the angels the "Progeny of Light" in Milton's *Paradise Lost*.

> *"The light that shines on the blessed angels is the supernatural knowledge of God's essence that is a gift of God's grace."*
> —*Mortimer Adler*

The angels' luminosity is attributed to the emanation of the Divine Light that becomes manifest in, and is emitted by them. In the fifteenth century, St. Francisca claimed to read her midnight prayers by the light that glowed from her guardian angel. And as embodiments of that sacred light, angels are thought to reflect the highest values of the Godhead.

> *"So far as the angels are recipients of that spiritual heat and light they are loves and wisdoms, not loves and wisdoms for themselves, but from the Lord."*
> —*Emanuel Swedenborg*

In the *Sefer Yezirah,* the Jewish Book of Creation, angels are said to be created from the four heavenly elements: mercy, strength, beauty, and dominion.

The seven angelic virtues mentioned elsewhere in Jewish thought are faith, wisdom, patience, mercy, judgment, peace, and goodness.

The Cabala describes ten "sefiroth"—abstract attributes of divine energy underlying creation, each of which is associated with angels: Foundation, Splendor, Eternity, Beauty, Power, Grace, Knowledge, Wisdom, Understanding, and Crown.

Many great poets have associated angels with particular noble qualities and virtues. William Shakespeare called angels "ministers of grace," and wrote of "reverence—that angel of the world," and of how "consideration like an angel came." John Milton wrote:

> *"O welcome pure-ey'd Faith, white-handed Hope,*
> *Thou hovering angels girt with golden wings."*

He also spoke of the "Cherub Contemplation," and of Wisdom, who, with Contemplation, "plumes her feathers, and lets grow her wings." And he described an angel full of compassion in his famous line, "Look homeward, Angel, now, and melt with ruth."

Henry Vaughan, the seventeenth-century English poet, described his childhood innocence as:

> *"Happy those early days, when I*
> *Shin'd in my angel-infancy."*

Alfred Lord Tennyson, England's poet laureate of the nineteenth century, wrote of a woman with "such angel grace." The nineteenth-century American poet Emily Dickinson, perhaps envisioning an angel, wrote that "hope is a thing with feathers."

A well-known African-American spiritual characterizes Ezekiel's vision of angel-like wheels:

> *"Ezekiel saw that wheel*
> *Way in the middle of the air.*
> *And the big wheel run by faith*
> *And the little wheel run by the Grace of God.*
> *A wheel within a wheel*
> *Way in the middle of the air."*

❧

Not one to overglorify the angels, William Blake complained that angels have no sense of humor, but his later countryman, writer G. K. Chesterton, quipped, "Angels can fly because they take themselves lightly."

The angelic attribute of superhuman physical strength is mentioned in many stories. In a Jewish legend, the Archangel Michael lifted Jerusalem into the air to protect it during the siege on that city by the Babylonian king Nebuchadnezzar. In the New Testament book of Revelation, four angels held back the four winds and "a mighty angel took up a stone like a great millstone and threw it into the sea . . ."

ORIGIN AND LIFESPAN OF THE ANGELS

Past scholars of both the Jewish and Christian traditions differ about when angels were first created by God. The Jewish text, the *Midrash ha-Ne'elam,* says that the angels "are the beginning of all created things, and were emanated from the splendor of His glorious light." As mentioned in Chapter 1, many thinkers include angels among the heavens created by God on the first day of creation.

> *"Where Scripture speaks of the world's creation, it is
> not plainly said whether or when the angels were created;
> but if mention is made, it is implicit under the name
> of 'heaven,' when it is said, 'In the beginning God
> created the heavens and the earth . . .' "*
> —St. Augustine

Other scholars offer arguments proposing either the second and/or fifth day.

These opinions usually reflect a notion that all of the angels ever created came into existence early in the history of time. And though angels had a finite beginning, and therefore were not considered eternal as God was, they were usually considered immortal and expected to live to the end of the ages.

> *"But you from the beginning were made spiritual,
> possessing a life . . . not subject to death."*
> —*God speaking to angels in the* Book of Enoch

Some angelologists have proposed that every new wish or desire of God automatically creates new angels to fulfill its accomplishment. One text says angels are formed "with every breath of God." Other scholars have suggested that there are two kinds of angels: some which live forever and some which have a lifespan limited to the duration of their specific duty or service.

Some philosophical thinkers of the west—reflecting views more commonly held in eastern thought—have proposed that the essential soul of a being grows and evolves toward a complete experience of all of life through a succession of many lifetimes and lifeforms. The Greek theologian Origen was one scholar who believed that the angels, following this pattern, die and are reborn into spiritually higher lifetimes. Some writers of the cabalic tradition also teach a similar idea. Emanuel Swedenborg, the Swedish mystic, wrote that "angels have been men" and are now living in a form closer to the nature of God.

GENDER AND SEXUALITY OF ANGELS

Given the human fascination with the topic of sexuality, it is only natural that the gender and sexual inclination of angels is a contested subject.

It would seem that if we take angels to be purely spiritual, bodiless beings, then they should be without gender. The cabalic work the *Zohar* says, "Angels . . . turn themselves into different shapes, being sometimes female and sometimes male."

Angels in traditional scripture are almost always described in masculine terms and referred to by the pronoun "he." This has sometimes created a rather chauvinistic attitude about the gender of all angels. John Wesley wrote about a servant girl who said she had seen an angel clothed in white, "glistening like silver" and "unspeakably musical," who foretold to her certain events which came to pass. Upon questioning her about her experience, Wesley said that he was "soon convinced that she was not only sincere, but deep in grace; and therefore incapable of deceit." Wesley was troubled, though, that the girl identified the angel as female, but excused her by saying that "from the face, the voice, and the apparel, she might easily mistake him for a female . . ."

There is one specific reference, however, to female winged beings in the Old Testament book of Zechariah, in which that prophet says, "Then I lifted my eyes and saw, and behold, two women coming forward! The wind was in their wings; they had wings like the wings of a stork, and they lifted up the ephah between heaven and earth."

Gabriel is often depicted in works of art in a feminine image and is often associated with "feminine" traits like beauty and grace. But Gabriel (not "Gabriella") is rarely specifically mentioned as female.

The depiction of angels in art has varied over time from male to female to androgynous.

Jesus, quoted in two of the gospels, said that when the spiritually saved are resurrected from the dead "they neither marry nor are given in marriage, but are like the angels of heaven." This declaration has been interpreted by some to indicate that not only are angels physically genderless, but that there are no sexual impulses in heaven. The Jewish philosopher Philo said that angels "never felt any craving after the things of earth." The contemporary American scholar Mortimer Adler stated, "Since angels are purely spiritual beings, they cannot have any passions or bodily desires." And in the Jewish *Book of Enoch,* God explains to the angels called the Watchers, "I made not wives for you, because, being spiritual, your dwelling is in heaven."

But, according to tradition, two hundred Watchers came to earth to satisfy their sexual attraction to the daughters of men.

And the Islamic heaven is said to be populated by female beings called *huris,* who provide erotic delights for the male Moslems who arrive there.

Emanuel Swedenborg, himself twice rejected in earthly proposals of marriage, wrote that the angels with whom he communed married and had homes together. And in Milton's *Paradise Lost* the Archangel Raphael describes to Adam and Eve the effortless coupling of angels:

> *"Whatever pure thou in the body enjoy'st*
> *(And pure thou wert created) we enjoy*
> *In eminence, and obstacle find none*

Of membrane, joint, or limb, exclusive bars:
Easier than air with air; if Spirits embrace,
Total they mix, union of pure with pure
Desiring, no restrained conveyance need
As flesh to mix with flesh, or soul with soul."

❁

ANGELIC NATURE AND HUMAN POTENTIAL

"Every man contemplates an angel in his future self."
—Ralph Waldo Emerson

Earlier in this chapter, a quote from Thomas Aquinas read, "There is a more perfect intellectual life in the angels." The New Testament writer Peter says that angels, compared to humans, "are greater in might and power." The author of the fifty-first of *The Federalist* papers, thought to be either Alexander Hamilton or James Madison, wrote, "If men were angels, no government would be necessary." And we popularly credit the angels with exceptional moral virtue when compared to humans—the living embodiment of the most glorious attributes of Divinity: Love, Beauty, Grace, Strength, Wisdom, Mercy, Peace, Truth, Judgment, Faith, Hope, Joy, and Humility, among others.

Though humans seem to come up short in these comparisons, it is significant that there even exists this common tendency to compare ourselves to the qualities of the angels. For in admiring the nature of angels, are we not venerating the best parts of ourselves? Perhaps as humans, we have within us what Abraham Lincoln called "the better angels of our nature"—the potential to become as magnificent an expression of life as the angels we imagine. For even in imagining the nature of angels, we are drawing from ideas that already exist within ourselves, within the range of human potential. By comparing ourselves to the angels, we reflect on our own better natures, our own capacity to experience a higher value of life.

> *"The soul at its highest is found like God, but an angel gives a closer idea of Him. That is all an angel is: an idea of God."*
> —*Johannes "Meister" Eckhart*

St. Paul, in his first letter to the Corinthians, writes of a day when humans shall have such discrimination that "we are to judge the angels." And the New Testament letter to the Hebrews says that God made humans only for "a little while lower than the angels." These epistles suggest that we all shall grow into a greater experience, wisdom, and understanding of life.

> *"Angels are spirits immaterial and intellectual, the glorious inhabitants of those sacred places where there is nothing but light and immortality; no shadow of matter for tears, discontentments, griefs, and uncomfortable passions to work upon; but all joy, tranquillity, and peace, even for ever and ever . . ."*
> —*Richard Hooker*

4 Pigeonholing the "birds of God" ~ Counting and categorizing the heavenly host

"Is there any number to his armies?"
—Job 25:3

he number of angels, their organization and subdivisions as a group, and their individual names and identities are long-standing topics of curiosity and fascination. For centuries, angel scholars attempted again and again to tally and categorize the angels—perhaps for no other reason than that it is the nature of scholars to want to quantify and systematize. Or perhaps because little scriptural authority or hard data exists from which to draw conclusive answers, angelologists feel compelled to try and provide their own solutions.

Though many learned heads have tried to count and catalog the heavenly host, there isn't any evidence to indicate that these undertakings have ever been done on anything other than an arbitrary basis. The results might even be what John Calvin, who disapproved of such endeavors, called "the vain babblings of idle men."

Even so, many scholars through the centuries acquired fame and notoriety for their calculations and explanations of the number, order, and names of the angels. So here is a potential arena of scholarship open to anyone aspiring to establish themselves as an authority of sorts. Only, as the dour Calvin warned, "Let those, who venture to determine concerning the multitude and orders of angels, examine on what foundation their opinions rest." For he thought that the knowledge of these things belongs "to that class of mysteries, the full revelation of which is deferred to the last day."

THE NUMBER OF ANGELS

> *"Of the Angels, th'exact number who*
> *Shall undertake to tell, he shall grow*
> *From Ignorance to Error; yet we may*
> *Conjecture."*
> *—Thomas Heywood*

Enoch, the Jewish patriarch and author of the book bearing his name, writes that in his trip to heaven he "beheld angels innumerable, thousands of thousands, and myriads and myriads." The New Testament author of the letter to the Hebrews speaks of the "innumerable angels in festal gathering" in "the heavenly Jerusalem." And the Koran states simply, "Numerous are the angels in heaven." From these sources we certainly get the idea that there are a lot of angels—"innumerable," uncountable. But something compels us to try to count them anyway.

In the Old Testament, Daniel saw in his vision of heaven that "a thousand thousands [i.e., millions] served him [God] and ten thousand times ten thousand [i.e., a hundred million] stood before him." That's a hundred million plus

more millions of angels, and those are just the ones in proximity to God in heaven.

John, the author of the book of Revelation in the New
Testament, heard "around the throne" the voices "of many
angels numbering myriads and myriads and thousands of
thousands."

An Islamic legend describes the Archangel Michael
(Mika'il, in Arabic) as covered from head to foot with hairs
of saffron. Each hair has a million faces, and each face a
million eyes. From each eye fall seven hundred thousand
tears, each of which becomes one of the cherubim. So just
computing the number of cherubim, only one of the orders
of angels, we have: 700,000 tears × 1,000,000 eyes ×
1,000,000 faces × all the hairs that cover Michael from
head to foot, or 700,000,000,000,000,000 (seven hundred
quadrillion) times the number of Michael's many hairs.
And that's just the number of cherubim.

Clement of Alexandria believed that stars are angels,
from which we would conclude that there are at least as
many angels as stars in the universe.

Simon ben Lakish of the third century took a census of
all the angels in the seven Jewish heavens, that he computed like this: For each of the twelve signs of the zodiac
there are thirty "hosts" of angels. Each host has thirty
"camps." Each camp has thirty "legions." Each legion has
thirty "cohorts." Each cohort has thirty "corps." Each
corps has three hundred thirty-five thousand "myriads."
Each myriad is comprised of ten thousand angels. Doing
our arithmetic now, that's $12 \times 30 \times 30 \times 30 \times 30 \times 30 \times$
$365,000 \times 10,000 = 1,064,340,000,000,000,000$, or 1.06434
quintillion angels. And that's a lot of angels.

Albert the Great, the thirteenth-century Dominican
monk, scholastic philosopher, and mentor of St. Thomas
Aquinas, numbered "each choir at 66,666 legions, and each

legion at 6,666 angels." That comes to 66,666 × 6,666, or 444,395,556 times the number of choirs, which in Albert's day was generally recognized as nine. So by his calculation, there are 3,999,560,004—or nearly 4 billion—angels.

Chapter 2 mentioned that Thomas Aquinas assigned one particular guardian angel to every human on earth. He also believed that only the lowest orders of angels serve humankind in this way. So, according to St. Thomas, there are many times more angels than the approximate number of 5.5 billion people living on the earth today.

Another calculation of the fourteenth century was made by a group of cabalists who computed the number of angels by "calculating words into numbers and numbers into words" and came up with the very exact number of 301,655,722—a paltry sum compared to the abovementioned accountings.

A CAUTION FOR ANGEL COUNTERS

Are any of these speculative calculations likely to be correct? Is it really relevant to count the number of angels at any one time?

Though the doctrine of the Roman Catholic Church holds that the number of angels was fixed at the time of creation, Origen—one of many who have questioned the constancy of the number of angels—thought that angels "multiply like flies." The *Zohar*, a book of the Cabala, mentions the six hundred million angelic messengers created on the second day of creation, but also says that angels were created on other days and for other purposes. Other scholars believed that every pronouncement of God results in the creation of new angels to facilitate the dispatch of God's wishes. Some Talmudic sages thought that every day a new batch of angels is created, praises God, and then sinks back into a great river of fire. Still others have hypothesized two kinds of angels: immortal angels and those created by God for a specific and limited purpose.

There is a well-known question that asks how many angels can dance on the head of a pin. This question is purported to be a typical "quodlibet," a theological or philosophical fine point over which scholars, particularly of the Middle Ages, quibbled.

The question is not asked to reveal some potent knowledge, but only to make those who try to comprehend the angels appear foolish. The question was never asked by medieval angelologists and is, as Mortimer Adler wrote, "simply one of the many modern inventions contrived to make a mockery of medieval thought."

THE HIERARCHY OF HEAVEN

"I arise today:
in the might of the Cherubim;
in the obedience of Angels;
in the ministration of Archangels ..."
—from the Lorica *of St. Patrick*

From the first speculation about angels there's been a presumption of a hierarchical organization among them. This is particularly true of Jewish and Christian lore, which have many times numbered and named the orders of angels and tried to clarify their differences.

CHRISTIAN HIERARCHY

The Roman Catholic Church has traditionally had a strong, centralized authority, which has supported a basically solid hierarchical organizational structure. Perhaps because of this the development of a recognized hierarchy of the angels within Christian belief was fairly homogeneous.

NAMES OF THE ORDERS

In the traditional Christian scheme, the names of the gradations or "choirs" of angels come from biblical references. The "seraphim" are mentioned twice in the Old Testament, "cherubim" many times. Michael is called "the archangel" in the book of Jude of the New Testament, and the word "angel" is used almost three hundred times in the Bible.

Other names are somewhat cryptically mentioned in the following segments of the New Testament letters of St. Paul to the Romans, Colossians, and Ephesians, respectively:

"For I am sure that neither death, nor life, nor angels, nor principalities, nor things present, nor things to come, nor powers, nor height, nor depth, nor anything else in all creation, will be able to separate us from the love of God in Christ Jesus our Lord."

"For in him all things were created, in heaven and on earth, visible and invisible, whether thrones or dominions or principalities or authorities . . ."

"He [God] raised him [Jesus] from the dead and made him sit at his right hand in the heavenly places, above all principality and power and virtue and dominion . . ."

Although it's not entirely clear from their context what St. Paul meant, the words "principalities," "powers," "thrones," "dominions" (often altered to "dominations"), and "virtues" were interpreted as specific references to the names of angelic orders.

THE HIERARCHY OF THE ORDERS

The "orthodox" number of choirs of angels in traditional Christian angelology is nine. St. Ambrose, the fourth-century bishop of Milan, was the first Church authority of note to propose a nine-tiered order. In his work *Apologia Prophet David* he gave as the names of the choirs in their descending order: Seraphim, Cherubim, Dominations,

Thrones, Principalities, Potentates (Powers), Virtues, Archangels, and Angels.

Pseudo-Dionysius arranged his angels in three orders of three choirs. The first order contained (in descending rank) Seraphim, Cherubim, and Thrones. The second order comprised Dominations, Virtues, and Powers. The third order included Principalities, Archangels, and Angels.

At the end of the sixth-century, pope, saint-to-be, and influential angelologist Gregory the Great certified the number of ranks of angels at nine, but transposed Principalities and Virtues in the order given by Pseudo-Dionysius. In his epic *The Divine Comedy*, Dante reconfirms the names and order given by Pseudo-Dionysius. And when Gregory arrives in Dante's heaven he sees for himself the errors of his transposition:

> *"These [the ranks of angels] once a mortal view beheld.*
>   *Desire,*
> *In Dionysius, so intensely wrought,*
> *That he, as I [Dante] have done, ranged them; and*
>   *named*
> *Their orders, marshaled in his thought. From him,*
> *Dissentient, one [Gregory] refused his sacred read;*
> *But soon as in this heaven his doubting eyes*
> *Were opened, Gregory at his error smiled."*

❊

St. Hildegarde, the twelfth-century founder and abbess of the Benedictine convent at Mt. St. Rupert in Germany, had visions of angels from the age of five, which she described in several books. St. Hildegarde has been regarded as a particularly credible mystic because she was a worldly and practical person. Her revelations about the celestial hierarchy also followed Dionysius' nine orders of angels.

In the thirteenth century St. Thomas Aquinas, in his

books *Summa Theologiae* and *Summa Contra Gentiles,* faithfully adopted the Dionysian three-by-three order, posing
and answering a series of questions regarding "the array of
angels," including:

1. "whether all the angels are in one hierarchy?"
2. "whether in one hierarchy there is just one order?"
3. "whether within one order there are many angels?"

Aquinas proposes the same ranking of angelic orders as
Dionysius and notes Gregory's switch of Principalities and
Virtues. But, he says, "to people who consider the matter
carefully the two ways of ordering them differ but slightly."

CHARACTERISTICS OF THE NINE TRADITIONAL ORDERS

Pseudo-Dionysius, Thomas Aquinas, Ambrose, Jerome,
and others have written of the distinctions of the different
orders of the angels. In general, the higher orders are presumed to be closer in their nature to God and to function
in roles that serve God more directly than the lower orders,
which tend to the administration of the physical universe
and the service of humankind. Some orders are associated
with particular divine qualities—Seraphim with Love,
Cherubim with Wisdom, Thrones with Judgment.

The Elizabethan playwright Thomas Heywood described
the orders of angels in a poem,

> *"The Seraphim doth in the word imply,*
> *A Fervent Love and Zeal to the Most-High . . .*
> *The Cherubim denotes to us the Fullness*
> *Of absolute Knowledge, free from Human dullness . . .*
> *The name of Thrones, his glorious Seat displays;*
> *His Equity and Justice, these still praise . . .*

Dominions, the Angels' offices dispose;
The Virtues (in the second place) are those
That execute his high and holy Will:
The Potentates they are assistant still,
The malice of the Devil to withstand:
For God hath given it to their powerful hand . . .
The Principates, of Princes take the charge,
Their power on earth to curb, or to enlarge;
And these work Miracles. The Arch-Angels are
Ambassadors, great matters to declare.
The Angels' commission hath not that extent,
They have only us Men in government."

✿

RECENT OPINIONS

Even into the twentieth century scholars still debate the certainty of angelic hierarchies. Rudolf Steiner was a German-speaking Czech who developed the Waldorf educational system and started a school of metaphysical thought he called Anthroposophy. Mr. Steiner described his own hierarchical system of nine orders, which had the names Seraphim, Cherubim, Thrones, Dominions, Mights, Powers, Archai, Archangels, and Angeloi or Angels.

In his book, *Angels: God's Secret Agents,* the contemporary evangelist Billy Graham proposed a ten-order hierarchy: Archangels, Angels, Seraphim, Cherubim, Principalities, Authorities, Powers, Thrones, Might, and Dominion.

Other names of angelic orders mentioned in various Christian angelologies include aeons, ambassadors, ardors, authorities, confessors, flames, governors, hosts, lordships, regents, sovereignties, voices, and warriors.

JEWISH HIERARCHY

Jewish scholarly opinion about the arrangement of angelic orders developed independently from Christian angelology and was more diverse.

NUMBER OF ORDERS

Traditionally there are seven heavens in the Jewish cosmology, and sometimes seven orders of angels were associated with this scheme. The *Book of Enoch* is often interpreted to name seven orders in this verse:

"He shall call to every power of the heavens, to all the holy above, and to the power of God. The Cherubim, the Seraphim, and the Ophanim, all the angels of power, all the angels of principalities, and the Elect One [the Messiah], and the other powers of the earth and over the water."

The Hebrew word "Ophanim" (Ofanim, Offannim) is sometimes thought synonymous with "Thrones," both of which are sometimes called "Wheels," after the description of angelic beings in Chapter 1 from Ezekiel in the Old Testament.

Other Jewish sources give different names and numbers to the angelic orders. In cabalistic thought, the ten Sefiroth, the divine attributes which underlie creation, are associated with ten orders of angels. The *Zohar* of the Cabala lists ten orders in descending rank—Arelim, Ishim, Bene Elohim, Malakim, Hashmallim, Tarshishim, Shinnanim, Cherubim, Ofanim, and Seraphim.

Moses Maimonides also proposed a ten-rank ordering with many of the names mentioned above: Hayyot, Ofanim, Arelim, Hashmallim, Seraphim, Malakim, Elohim, Bene Elohim, Cherubim, and Ishim.

But for the most part, descriptions of the angelic hierarchy in Jewish thought are inconsistent. *3 Enoch,* one of the most angel-filled books in all of Jewish literature, gives three different schemes of the celestial hierarchy.

Like ophanim and thrones, other Jewish orders have sometimes been thought synonymous with Christian orders. The hashmallim are sometimes equated with dominations, hayyots with the cherubim, and malakim or tarshishim with virtues.

The following lists show some of the variety of opinion over the centuries about the names and ranking of the angelic orders:

ORDERS OF THE ANGELS

St. Ambrose	*Gregory the Great*
1. Seraphim	1. Seraphim
2. Cherubim	2. Cherubim
3. Dominations	3. Thrones
4. Thrones	4. Dominations
5. Principalities	5. Principalities
6. Potentates (Powers)	6. Powers
7. Virtues	7. Virtues
8. Archangels	8. Archangels
9. Angels	9. Angels

Pseudo-Dionysius (and later St. Hildegarde,
St. Thomas Aquinas, and Dante)

1. Seraphim
2. Cherubim
3. Thrones (Wheels)
4. Dominations (Dominions)
5. Virtues
6. Powers
7. Principalities

8. Archangels
9. Angels

Rudolf Steiner
1. Seraphim
2. Cherubim
3. Thrones
4. Dominions
5. Mights
6. Powers
7. Archai
8. Archangels
9. Angels

Billy Graham
1. Archangels
2. Angels
3. Seraphim
4. Cherubim
5. Principalities
6. Authorities
7. Powers
8. Thrones
9. Might
10. Dominion

Enoch
1. Cherubim
2. Seraphim
3. Ofanim
4. All the angels of power
5. Principalities
6. The Elect One (Messiah)
7. The powers of earth and water

The Zohar
1. Arelim
2. Ishim
3. Bene Elohim
4. Malakim
5. Hashmallim
6. Tarshishim
7. Shinnanim

Moses Maimonides
1. Hayyot
2. Ofanim
3. Arelim
4. Hashmallim
5. Seraphim
6. Malakim
7. Elohim

8. Cherubim
9. Ofanim
10. Seraphim

8. Bene Elohim
9. Cherubim
10. Ishim

NAMES OF THE ANGELS

*"May Michael be at my right hand and Gabriel at
my left, before me Uriel and Raphael, and above my
head the divine presence of God."*
—*Jewish prayer*

The Jewish sect of the Essenes, which flourished at the
time of Jesus, imposed an oath on those entering the order
never to reveal the names of the angels. For in the knowledge of the names, they believed, was power that could be
abused, and that could distract the spiritual aspirant from
his principal reason for being a member of the community.

Though few angels are given names in the most conser-
vatively accepted religious scriptures, thousands of angels
are named in lesser-known works and in popular lore.
We'll take some time here to mention a few individual angels who are most prominent in scripture and legend.

ANGELS OF THE BIBLE

The Bible mentions three distinguished angels by
name—Michael, Gabriel, and Raphael.

MICHAEL (WHO IS AS GOD)

In the Old Testament book of Daniel, Michael is "one of
the chief princes" of the Hebrew people and later "your
prince," and then "the great prince who has charge over
your people." In the Dead Sea Scrolls, he is the "Prince of
Light." Of the seventy angel-princes set over the seventy
nations in Jewish thought, Michael is the protector of Is-

rael and is also chief among all of the angel-princes. In this role, as it is portrayed in art, Michael's symbol is the scepter.

In both Jewish and Christian lore, Michael sometimes assumes the role of warrior-angel. *2 Enoch* calls Michael "general" and "great captain." In the book of Daniel, Michael fights against the Persians. And in the book of Revelation in the New Testament, Michael leads the army of God's angels against the forces of Satan, defeating the Evil One in battle. Pope Leo XIII wrote a prayer to Michael the warrior-angel which says,

> *"Holy Michael archangel, defend us in the day of battle;*
> *be our safeguard against the wickedness and snares of the*
> *devil . . . and do thou, Prince of the heavenly host, by*
> *the power of God thrust down to hell Satan and all*
> *wicked spirits . . ."*

❈

Michael was often depicted in Christian art as an armor-clad fighter wielding a mighty broadsword and shield, or a great lance. His symbol is the sword.

In Christian belief, Michael is sometimes thought to be the Lord of Souls who judges the souls of the dead and conducts the spirits of the just to heaven. In this role, his symbol in art is the scales. He also hears the prayers and supplications of humankind.

It was the angel Michael who appeared kneeling and holding a burning taper to the Virgin to tell her of her approaching death. Michael is an angel of repentance, righteousness, mercy, and sanctification.

In Jewish tradition he is also classified as one of the seven archangels—sometimes said to be the chief archangel—and one of the four angels stationed at the sides of the throne of God.

As the guardian angel of the Hebrew nation in the Judaic tradition, Michael is sometimes thought to be synonymous with the "angel of the Lord" who appears in the tales of the Torah to succor Hagar in the wilderness, restrain Abraham from sacrificing Isaac, bring the plagues on Egypt, and lead the Israelites in their Exodus.

Jewish legends say that God spoke to Moses through the mouth of Michael in the Burning Bush, and that Michael carried the tablets to Moses on Mt. Sinai. In another story, Satan tried to enter the lifeless body of Moses when Moses died to deceive the Jews and confuse them. But Michael contended with Satan for the body of Moses, defeated him, and secretly buried the body in a hidden place.

The *Book of Enoch* calls Michael "the merciful, the patient, the holy," and says that he presides over human virtue and commands all nations.

Michael (Mika'il, in Arabic) is also prominent in Islamic angelology, where he dwells in the seventh Moslem heaven.

He is the Islamic angel of food and knowledge. In Egypt, Michael is patron of the Nile, and his feast is celebrated each year on the day the river rises.

During the plague that devastated sixth-century Rome, Michael is said to have appeared hovering over the city with a drawn sword on the day Gregory the Great was invested as pope. The archangel touched down on the top of the Mausoleum of Hadrian and sheathed his sword, which dripped with blood. And from that hour the plague vanished from the city. The Mausoleum was subsequently topped with a statue of the archangel and called the Castle of Sant'Angelo.

Michael also appeared twice to command the building of Christian churches. One, at Monte Gargano on the east coast of Italy, became a place of pilgrimage for the curative waters that were discovered at the site. According to one version of the legend, a wealthy fifth-century cattle owner named Gargano, accompanied by his servants, was searching for a stray bull. The men finally found the errant animal near the top of a mountain, standing by the mouth of a cave. Gargano was angry at the bull for causing them to worry and search for it, and he ordered one of his servants to shoot the bull with a bow and arrow. Inexplicably, the arrow turned in mid-flight and pierced the man who shot it. Troubled and mystified by this strange event, Gargano sent for the local bishop to ask for an explanation of what had occurred. The bishop fasted and prayed for three days, at which time Michael appeared to him and said that the spot where the bull stood by the cave was sacred ground and that the archangel had intervened to prevent a defiling of the soil. Then Michael instructed the bishop to build a church on the spot where the bull had stood.

A second church, at Avranches, a tiny island off the coast of Normandy, in France, was erected at Michael's instruction when he appeared to St. Aubert, the local bishop. At first the bishop thought he was dreaming and disregarded Michael's direction. So Michael appeared a second and third time to St. Aubert, finally placing a mark on Aubert's head to convince him that the angel and his petition were no dream. The small church that was first constructed on the famous site was later replaced by a larger, more beautiful abbey, which still stands today.

St. Michael is the patron saint of Brittany, Cornwall, Germany, Papua, New Guinea, and of marines and paratroopers. The Church of England and the American Episcopal Church celebrate Michaelmas, the feast of St. Michael, on September 29. As recently as 1950, Pope Pius XII declared Michael the official patron of policemen.

Michael also came to the aid of Christian, the protagonist of seventeenth-century English writer John Bunyan's *Pilgrim's Progress*, during his battle with the fiend Appolyon:

> *"Therefore to him let me give lasting praise*
> *And thank and bless his holy name always."*

GABRIEL (HERO OF GOD)

Gabriel is the messenger angel who appeared to the Virgin Mary and to Muhammad—"Heaven's Golden-winged Herald." In Christian tradition, Gabriel is the angel of annunciation, heavenly mercy, resurrection, and revelation. It is Gabriel who will blow the horn announcing the second coming of Christ. In Islam, Gabriel is the Angel of Humanity, the spirit of truth, and the prince of the guardian angels. In Jewish belief he is chief of the angelic guards and the keeper of the celestial treasury.

Sufi Ruzbehan Baqli describes him:

"I saw Gabriel, like a maiden, or like the moon amongst the stars. His hair was like a woman's, falling in long tresses. He wore a red robe embroidered in green ... He is the most beautiful of Angels ... His face is like a red rose."

❧

In his poem *The Golden Moon,* Longfellow calls Gabriel the angel of the moon, who brings humankind the gift of hope.

Gabriel is frequently depicted in art, especially Christian art, and his symbol is the lily. In Christian scripture Gabriel announced the impending births of Jesus and John the Baptist. In apocryphal legends he also foretold the births of Samson and of the Virgin Mary. Perhaps by virtue of his association with these annunciations, Gabriel is regarded as the angel who presides over childbirth.

In Jewish literature Gabriel, like Michael, is one of the seven archangels and one of the four throne angels. He is the angel of judgment, presiding "over all that is powerful."

Origen, in his third-century treatise on angels, assigned Gabriel the job of "the direction of wars," and Gabriel was second-in-command of God's army in Milton's description of the war in heaven.

In Moslem legends, Gabriel delivered the Black Stone of the Kaba to Abraham in Mecca, which, to this day, is kissed by pilgrims during the annual haj (pilgrimage) to that holy city. According to legend, the archangel dug the never-diminishing Well of Zamzam in Mecca for use by Hagar and Ishmael when they were dying of thirst in the wilderness. And, riding a pure white horse, Gabriel fought with Muhammad and his victorious Islamic troops in 624 A.D. at the Battle of Bedr against a far superior force of infidel soldiers.

More recently, Father Rapp, the leader of a German religious sect that established a community on the Wabash River in the nineteenth century, claimed he saw Gabriel in the forest and that the archangel "had the good taste to leave footprints behind." The commune is long gone, but the impression of a footprint preserved in limestone in New Harmony, Indiana, still recalls Gabriel's visit.

In his role as announcer of tidings, Gabriel is the patron of messengers and postal employees. In 1951, Pope Pius XII declared Gabriel the patron angel of telecommunications workers.

RAPHAEL (GOD HEALS)

Raphael is noted in Jewish and Christian literature as an archangel and one of the throne angels. In Christian belief he is chief of the guardian angels and has the special task of protecting the young, the innocent, and pilgrims and other travelers.

In Longfellow's play "The Nativity," Raphael says,

> *"I am the Angel of the Sun*
> *Whose flaming wheels began to run*
> *When God's almighty breath*
> *Said to the darkness and the Night,*
> *Let there be light! and there was light*
> *I bring the gift of Faith."*

❖

Raphael is the angel of prayer, love, joy, light, providence, and, especially, healing. In the *Book of Enoch*, Raphael is "set over all the diseases and all the wounds of the children of men," and is "he who presides over every suffering and every affliction of the sons of men." Origen assigned to Raphael "the work of caring and healing." And the *Zohar* says that "Raphael is charged to heal the earth, and through him . . . the earth furnishes an abode for man, whom also he heals of his maladies."

In Christian lore, Raphael warns Adam of the danger of sin, which Milton portrays in *Paradise Lost:*

> *"Be strong, live happy, and love! but first of all*
> *Him whom to love is to obey, and keep*
> *His great command; take heed lest passion sway*
> *Thy judgment to do aught, which else free-will*
> *Would not admit; thine and of all thy sons*
> *The weal or woe in thee is placed; beware!"*

❧

In traditional legends, Raphael is best known from his role in the *Book of Tobit,* where he serves as a guardian, guide, matchmaker, teacher, healer, and companion to Tobias and his family. Most paintings of Raphael are taken from scenes in *Tobit.* In Christian iconography, Raphael's symbol is the pilgrim's staff. He is the patron angel of the blind, of happy meetings, and of nurses, physicians, and travelers.

In Milton's *Paradise Lost,* Adam, speaking to a departing Raphael, says,

> *"Go, Heavenly Guest, Ethereal Messenger,*
> *Sent from whose sovran goodness I adore!*
> *Gentle to me and affable hath been*
> *Thy condescension, and shall be honoured ever*
> *With grateful memory. Thou to Mankind*
> *Be good and friendly still, and oft return!"*

❧

OTHER ANGELS

Of the angels around the throne, in addition to Michael, Gabriel, and Raphael, the fourth is said to be Uriel, or sometimes Phanuel.

Uriel means "Fire of God." In both Jewish and Christian lore Uriel is one of the angels placed by God "at the east of Eden" to "guard the way to the tree of life." Milton calls him the "sharpest sighted spirit of all in Heaven," and pictures him "gliding through the even/On a sunbeam, swift as a shooting star." Uriel is associated with light and is the angel of illumination and interpretation. In works of art, Uriel often carries a scroll.

There is one other angel mentioned by name in the Bible. The New Testament book of Revelation refers to "the angel of the bottomless pit; his name in Hebrew is Abaddon, and in Greek he is called Apollyon."

Historic lists of the seven archangels always include the names of Michael, Gabriel, and Raphael. The other four vary in name by source. What seems to be the earliest recorded reference to the archangels is the Ethiopic *Enoch,* which lists Uriel, Raguel, Zerachiel, and Remiel. Pseudo-Dionysius specified Uriel, Chamuel, Jophiel, and Zadkiel. Gregory the Great included Uriel, Simiel, Orifiel, and Zachariel. Thomas Heywood cited Chamuel, Adabiel, Haniel, and Zaphiel.

Several contemporary New Age angelologists have stated their belief in twelve—not seven—archangels and name them as Michael, Gabriel, Raphael, Uriel, Chamuel, Jophiel, Zadkiel, Aquariel, Anthriel, Valeoel, Perpetiel, and Omniel.

Names of individual angels have commonly been associated with the twelve signs of the zodiac, with each of the planets, and with the four seasons, days of the moon cycle, days of the week, hours of the day, and points of the compass.

Metatron, with seventy-two mystical names, is often mentioned as the highest-ranking angel in Jewish lore—the prince of all angels, the chancellor of heaven. He is the ruling angel of the Seventh Hall, the innermost and holiest sanctum, the true abode of God. He is sometimes called the Prince of the Presence or Angel of the Face because, in some Jewish traditions, he alone has access to the Divine Presence of the Godhead.

Metatron is the angel of the covenant, head of the celestial academy, and holds the keys to the light of illumination and the light of discernment. He is the prince of mysteries and controls all the secret treasuries of hidden wisdom.

In scripture, Metatron is often referred to as "na'ar," the Hebrew word for boy, or lad, because he is constantly rejuvenated and reborn into a profound spiritual awareness.

A Jewish legend says that Metatron's "height and his breadth became equal to the height and breadth of the world, and thirty-six wings were attached to his body . . . and 365,000 eyes were bestowed upon him, each brilliant as the sun."

Just prior to the Flood, the prophet Enoch was transported—while still alive—directly to heaven and transformed, first into an angel, and then into the angel-prince Metatron. In *3 Enoch* he describes his transformation:

"Forthwith my flesh was changed into flames, my sinews into flaming fire, my bones into coals of burning juniper, the light of my eyelids into splendor of lightnings, my eyeballs into firebrands, the hair of my head into hot flames, all of my limbs into wings of burning fire, and the whole of my body into glowing fire."

The Jewish prophet Elijah was transformed into the great angel Sandalphon, who exceeds the height of all other angels "by the length of a journey of five hundred years." Sandalphon is an angel-prince—the twin brother of Metatron and a master of heavenly song.

In Jewish lore, Sandalphon gathers the prayers of the faithful and weaves them into a garland, which he presents to God. Longfellow's poem "Sandalphon" calls him the Angel of Glory and Angel of Prayer, and says:

> *". . . he gathers the prayers as he stands,*
> *And they change into flowers in his hands,*
> *Into garlands of purple and red."*

❊

In Moslem folklore, Israfel is "the burning one," the angel of resurrection and music, who will sound the trumpet on the Day of Judgment. Israfel places souls in bodies, and he is thought to have served as Muhammad's companion and spiritual initiator for three years before Gabriel came to command Muhammad to recite the Koran.

In Islamic lore, Azrael was the only angel who was able to gather the handfuls of dust that Allah used to create Adam. Azrael is the Moslem and Hebrew angel of death. Legend says that he has 70,000 eyes and 4,000 wings, and his body has "as many eyes and tongues as there are men in the world." Each time an eye closes, someone dies.

5 ~ Feathers and light
The appearance of angels and their images in art

> "It is to those who perceive through symbols, the poets, the artists, and seekers for meaning, that the angel makes himself known."
> —Theodora Ward

So far we've covered a variety of thoughts and beliefs about angels: what they are, what they do, what they're like, how many there are, and how they're organized. Certain of these concepts will resonate with you more than others—some you will embrace, some you'll reject, others may be set aside for further consideration. Eventually you will come to your own unique understanding about angels and what they mean to you.

This understanding, or idea, of an angel gives rise in the inner vision—in the imagination—to a representation that makes manifest that idea. Your imagination creates a picture, a visual symbol, embodying the attributes of the idea.

Those with an artistic nature might wish to bring forth that image of angels in a painting, or in sculpture, or in the words of a poem. And, a picture being worth a thousand

words, the sensory experience of the image acts to restim-
ulate, expand, and enrich the original thought or idea.

So the idea and the image, the archetype and the icon,
of angels go hand in hand. And, because the idea of angels
is such a long-standing and significant one to the human
mind, it has inspired the creation of thousands of images
over many centuries. In fact, few, if any, other subjects in
the history of art have inspired so many artists and ap-
pealed to so great an audience as the images of angels.

> *"Perhaps there are no artistic representations that appeal
> to a greater number of people, of all possible types, than
> do those of angels ..."*
> —Clara Erskine Waters

John Ruskin, the nineteenth-century English art critic,
believed that the noblest use to which humans can employ
their imagination is "to bring sensibly to our sight the
things which are recorded as belonging to our future state,
or as invisibly surrounding us in this. It [imagination] is
given us that we may imagine the cloud of witnesses in
heaven and earth ... that we may conceive the great army
of the inhabitants of heaven, and discover among them
those who we most desire to be with forever; that we may
be able to vision forth the ministry of angels beside us, and
see the chariots of fire on the mountains that gird us
round ..."

So for nearly 3,000 years artists grand and humble have
sought to express within the range of the senses what is
usually beyond the senses—bringing into being images that
can only be realized through the power of imagination.

ANGELS DESCRIBED IN SCRIPTURE

Most people today would quickly be able to identify angels as the winged, haloed, white-robed, flowing-haired, anthropomorphic beings depicted in religious and secular art. But where did this image come from? Does it faithfully represent angels? Is it significant to us as a symbol?

The English cleric John Wesley wrote that "we have in general only a faint and indistinct perception of their [the angels'] presence." Though we think of angels as spiritual beings and servants of God, there are few details of the appearance of angels given in traditional religious scripture. Those descriptions that do exist, though, are powerful and mysterious and worth sharing here.

Ezekiel's vision

In the book of Ezekiel in the Old Testament, the prophet describes his vision of two kinds of other-worldly beings. The first kind, which appeared to Ezekiel from out of a cloud, he calls "living creatures."

> *"I knew that they were cherubim, and this was their appearance: they had the form of men, but each had four faces, and each of them had four wings. Their legs were straight, and the soles of their feet were like the sole of a calf's foot; and they sparkled like burnished bronze. Under their wings on their four sides they had human hands. And the four had their faces and their wings thus: their wings touched one another; and they went everyone straight forward, without turning as they went.*
>
> *"As for the likeness of their faces, each had the face of a man in front; the four had the face of a lion on the right side, the four had the face of an ox on the left side, and the four had the face of an eagle at the back. Such were their faces.*

> *"And their wings were spread out above; each creature
> had two wings, each of which touched the wing of another;
> while two covered their bodies. And each went straight
> forward; wherever the spirit would go, they went, without
> turning as they went."*

❈

In this same vision, Ezekiel also describes the second
kind of being, which he calls "wheels," thought by some
angel scholars to represent the angelic order of powers, or
thrones:

> *"Now as I looked at the living creatures, I saw a wheel
> upon the earth beside the living creatures, one for each of
> the four of them. As for the appearance of the wheels
> and their construction: their appearance was like the
> gleaming of a chrysolite; and the four had the same likeness,
> their construction being as it were a wheel within a wheel.
> When they went, they went in any of their four directions
> without turning as they went. The four wheels had rims
> and they had spokes; and their rims were full of eyes round
> about."*

❈

Later Ezekiel says more about the wheels:

> *"And their rims, and their spokes, and the wheels were
> full of eyes all round about—the wheels that the four of
> them had. As for the wheels, they were called in my
> hearing the whirling wheels. And every one had four
> faces: the first face was the face of the cherub, and the second
> face was the face of a man, and the third the face of a
> lion, and the fourth the face of an eagle."*

❈

Ezekiel also recounts how these two kinds of beings he has described—the cherubim and the wheels—appeared to be associated together:

> *"And when the living creatures went, the wheels went beside them; and when the living creatures rose from the earth, the wheels rose. Wherever the spirit would go, they went, and the wheels rose along with them; for the spirit of the living creatures was in the wheels. When those went, these went; and when those stood, these stood; and when those rose from the earth, the wheels rose along with them; for the spirit of the living creatures was in the wheels."*

❖

Here, in short, is Ezekiel's biblical description of cherubim and wheels (powers): The cherubim have "the form of men," but with four faces and four wings, and an appearance that "sparkled like burnished bronze." The other beings are "whirling wheels," with "rims and spokes" and "full of eyes all round about," shining like "the gleaming of a chrysolite," and "their construction being as it were a wheel within a wheel."

OTHER BIBLICAL DESCRIPTIONS

In the Old Testament, Daniel describes an angel who appeared to him:

> *"I lifted up my eyes and looked, and behold, a man clothed in linen, whose loins were girded with gold of Uphaz. His body was like beryl, his face like the appearance of lightning, his eyes like flaming torches, his arms and*

legs like the gleam of burnished bronze, and the sound of his words like the noise of a multitude."

❖

The Old Testament prophet Isaiah briefly mentions the appearance of seraphim, each with six wings:

"And above him [the Lord] stood the seraphim; each had six wings: with two he covered his face, and with two he covered his feet, and with two he flew."

❖

And John, the author of Revelation, describes four "living creatures" thought to represent the throne angels:

"And round the throne, on each side of the throne, are four living creatures, full of eyes in front and behind: the first living creature like a lion, the second living creature like an ox, the third living creature with the face of a man, and the fourth living creature like a flying eagle. And the four living creatures, each of them with six wings, are full of eyes all round and within, and day and night they never cease to sing . . ."

❖

This last description seems like a composite of the visions of Ezekiel and Isaiah. John terms the beings he saw "living creatures," as Ezekiel did. The four creatures in John, being like a lion, an ox, a man, and an eagle, respectively, correspond to the appearance of the four faces of Ezekiel's cherubim. John's creatures are "full of eyes all round and within," similar to the eyes of Ezekiel's wheels, or powers. John's angels also have the six wings of the seraphim noted by Isaiah.

Later in Revelation, John describes another angel:

"Then I saw another mighty angel coming down from heaven, wrapped in a cloud, with a rainbow over his head, and his face was like the sun, and his legs like pillars of fire. He had a little scroll open in his hand. And he set his right foot on the sea, and his left foot on the land, and called out with a loud noise, like a lion roaring; when he called out, the seven thunders sounded."

❧

ANTHROPOMORPHIC ANGELS

The cherubim seen by Ezekiel "had the form of men." Daniel calls the being he saw "a man clothed in linen." But Ezekiel's wheels, or powers, seem very differently formed, and the creatures described by John surrounding God's throne have more the appearance of animals than humans. Still, even without a consistent and universal description given in scripture or elsewhere, representations of angels are almost always based on the form of humans. There is, however, some scriptural authority given by angel scholars to justify this idea. In Genesis, God speaks to an unnamed audience, presumed by some to be an angel or many angels, saying, "Let us make man in our image, after our likeness." In this interpretation, God has decided to make humans in the image of not only him/herself, but of the angels, to whom God is thought to be speaking.

St. Thomas Aquinas wrote, "Hence it is that the Lord promises men the glory of the angels: 'They shall be,' He says, speaking of men, 'like the angels of God in heaven' [Matthew 22:30]. And also it is said that there is 'the same measure for man and for angel' [Revelation 21:17]. For this reason, too, almost everywhere in Sacred Scripture angels are described in the shape of men: either wholly, as is evident of the angels who appeared to Abraham in the likeness of men [Genesis 18:2]; or partially, as is the case of the

animals of who it is said that 'they had the hands of a man under their wings.' [Ezekiel 1:8]."

FACT OR FANTASY?

In Chapter 1 we discussed whether angels have bodies at all and, if so, whether they are temporary, "assumed bodies" or permanent physiques. The question of whether or not angels truly have an anthropomorphic form is usually answered in one of three ways, depending on whom you ask:

1. Angels do have a kind of form similar to humans.
2. Angels have no permanent form, but choose to reveal themselves to humans in a humanlike appearance to facilitate our understanding and acceptance of them.
3. It is only flattering and erroneously reassuring for humans to represent angels as appearing like ourselves, with the addition of a few extra features to which we might aspire: wings, a halo, and radiance.

"We cannot think of angels as a reality in the winged, human forms that have been given them in Art, any more than we can look for mermaids to rise from the waters mentioned in the charming legends in which these maidens acted their parts. These imaginary and apparently palpable angels are but allegories, which long have been and continue to be the angels of Art, and we could not willingly give them up. We know that they are impossible, even fantastic, if we permit ourselves to be matter-of-fact; but as emblems of spiritual guardians, sent to mortals by an ever-watchful Father, we love them . . ."
—Clara Erskine Waters

Clearly, Ms. Waters' opinion is of the third variety described above, but it is worth keeping in mind that most myths and legends have at least a seed of truth to them. And this seed of truth is part of what endears an image to a place in the human heart. A thirteenth-century poem by the Persian poet Rumi depicts the Archangel Gabriel speaking to the Virgin Mary:

> *"Look well, for I am a Form difficult to discern.*
> *I am a new moon, I am an Image in the heart.*
> *When an Image enters your heart and establishes itself,*
> *you flee in vain: the Image will remain within you—*
> *unless it is a vain fancy without substance,*
> *sinking and vanishing like a false dawn.*
> *But I am like the true dawn, I am the Light of your*
> *Lord . . ."*

❖

Artists—and western culture as a whole—have traditionally chosen a likeness of humans to represent angels, and we do, as Clara Erskine Waters says, cherish this representation. So, at least as a visual symbol of the idea of angel, this image has meaning and purpose and power.

> *"The image of the Angel in art emerges from a creative*
> *interplay between traditional canons—based on Scripture—and*
> *the personal vision of the artist. To say that a visionary*
> *sees what Scripture and sacred art have prepared him*
> *to see is not to accuse him of inauthenticity; vision is real,*
> *but it is also influenced by culture. In the resonances created*
> *by this paradox, the Angel unveils itself."*
>
> —Peter L. Wilson

THE HISTORY OF ANGELS IN ART
"For now I have seen the angel of the Lord face to face."
—Judges 6:22

The history of angels in art is a significant topic in its own right and could be the subject of its own lengthy volume, richly illustrated with examples of paintings, drawings, and sculpture of many notable masters, including Fra Angelico, Leonardo da Vinci, Michelangelo, Titian, Raphael, El Greco, Rubens, Van Dyck, Velasquez, Rembrandt, Delacroix, Blake, Manet, Gauguin, Van Gogh, and Chagall. They and thousands of other artistic visionaries have produced a fantastic quantity of extraordinary images of angels.

One of the earliest works of art considered by scholars to represent an angel was excavated at the ancient Sumerian city of Ur, the Old Testament's first home of Abraham. Sculpted on a stele is a winged figure flying down from heaven and holding a jar of overflowing water, which is thought to symbolize the power of God and life. The angel pours the water into the cup of an earthly king, who personifies humankind.

Since this early image, representations of angels in art have generally changed over time, reflecting the evolution of human belief about them and changes in the culture as a whole. As emissaries of God, angels have evolved symbolically as our belief in a Supreme Being has changed from the heavy-handed autocrat of the early Old Testament, to the poetic Divinity of the Psalms, to the merciful and personally caring Father of the early Christians. As God and heaven became more remote from us in religious thought, the angels became a more tangible manifestation of purity and grace, and stood in for God as objects of love and reverence, appreciated for their beauty and protective guardianship. When the Protestant reformation urged its adherents to spurn symbols and base their relationship with God only on the biblical Word, angels were mostly relegated to their association with biblical stories. With the growth of scientific thought during the eighteenth and nineteenth centuries, we moved even farther away from our angelic heritage. But today there is a new and growing closeness to the angels—one that is not strictly associated with traditional religion.

Angels in art are at times depicted as mature beings, sometimes as youths, sometimes as children, sometimes as chubby, winged babies—or "putti," as they're called. In the earliest mosaics and paintings depicting biblical stories, angels appear as mature men. Byzantine angels take on the faces and bodies of young men, but also seem to project an air of authority. Romanesque angels seem younger, and perhaps more lively. Gothic angels have a look of innocent youth. By the sixteenth century, angels often appear as children, or babies, or even as only an infant head with wings.

Through the thirteenth century, paintings of angels exhibit a predominantly masculine appearance. Over the next three hundred years, their images become more delicate, gentle, and feminine, until angels are shown as androgynous or even distinctly female. Since the seventeenth century, the visual expression of angels has been less influenced by the tenets of the times and more open to the personal interpretation of the individual artist.

Sometimes angels in art look solemn—even stern—other times light and gay. In general, however, the appearance of command and authority in the earliest representations of angels gave way to images of innocence, sweetness, grace, and joy.

Sometimes angels are portrayed as colossal in size, sometimes human-sized, sometimes diminutive. At times they appear all too human; others are breathtakingly ethereal.

Angels in art can portray emotional expression ranging from the ecstasy and adoration of God, to the rage and fury of warriors in righteous battle, to the anguish of deep loss and sorrowful mourning.

SUBJECTS OF ART DEPICTING ANGELS

Angels have been prominent subjects during some of the most prolific and creative eras in western art. A number of traditional scenes depicting angels have been interpreted over and over again by painters and sculptors, especially in the Christian art of the Middle Ages and the Renaissance. These subjects come from both well-known biblical and popular stories. From the Old Testament these scenes include:

- Abraham deterred by an angel from sacrificing Isaac;
- the visit of the three angels to Abraham;
- Hagar in the wilderness being instructed by the angel to return to Abraham and Sarah;
- Jacob's dream (Jacob's ladder);
- Jacob wrestling with an angel;
- the angel comforting Elijah;
- the vision of Ezekiel;
- the rescue of Shadrach, Meshach, and Abednego from the fiery furnace;
- the protection of Daniel in the lion's den;
- the expulsion of Adam and Eve from the Garden of Eden; and
- Raphael and Tobias from the *Book of Tobit.*

Often-painted New Testament scenes involving angels include:

- the annunciation to Zechariah by Gabriel of the coming birth of John the Baptist;
- the Annunciation to the Virgin Mary by Gabriel of the coming birth of Jesus;
- the angel announcing the birth of Jesus to the shepherds near Bethlehem;
- Joseph's dream of the angel;
- angels ministering to John the Baptist in the wilderness;
- angels ministering to Jesus in the wilderness;
- the angel comforting Jesus in the Agony in the Garden of Gethsemane;
- the women and the angel at the sepulcher of Jesus;
- St. Peter freed from prison by an angel;
- the angel smiting Herod;
- Michael subduing Satan in the battle of heaven.

Though not a scene mentioned in the Bible, the annunciation of the death of the Virgin by the Archangel Michael has also been frequently painted.

There are many traditional scenes in which angels are not the primary characters, but are often used in subsidiary roles—especially scenes from the life of Jesus. These include:

- the Nativity;
- the Adoration of the Magi;
- the Madonna and Child;
- the Flight of Joseph, Mary, and Jesus into Egypt;
- the Repose in Egypt;
- the Baptism of Jesus;

- the Passion of Jesus;
- the Crucifixion of Jesus;
- the Pietà;
- the Coronation of the Virgin—showing the reunion of the Mother and Son in heaven;
- the Enthroned Madonna;
- the Last Judgment.

THE RADIANCE OF ANGELS

The whiteness and brightness characteristic of angels in art and poetry attest to their purity and spiritual radiance. Their truest colors are white and gold; they gleam and shine.

> *"We trust, in plumed procession,*
> *For such the angels go,*
> *Rank after rank, with even feet*
> *And uniforms of snow."*
> *—Emily Dickinson*

Ezekiel the prophet saw angels who "sparkled like burnished bronze," with "the gleaming of a chrysolite," and they moved "like a flash of lightning." And the angel that Daniel saw had loins "girded with gold of Uphaz," a face "like the appearance of lightning," eyes "like flaming torches," and limbs "like the gleam of burnished bronze." The "mighty angel" described by John had a "face like the sun" and "legs like pillars of fire."

> *"They had their faces all of living flame*
> *And wings of gold and all the rest so white*
> *That never snow has known such purity."*
> *—Dante*

In the New Testament, Matthew writes of the angel who spoke to the women at Jesus' tomb: "his appearance was like lightning, and his raiment white as snow." And in Revelation, John "saw another angel coming down from heaven, having great authority; and the earth was made bright with his splendor."

> *"The helmed Cherubim*
> *And sworded Seraphim,*
> *Are seen in glittering ranks with wings display'd."*
> —John Milton

In describing his transformation from man to angel, the *Book of Enoch* tells how the prophet was changed from "flesh to fire" and then "clothed with light and splendor."

> *"Their garments are white, but with an unearthly whiteness.*
> *I cannot describe it, because it cannot be compared to earthly*
> *whiteness; it is much softer to the eye. These bright*
> *Angels are enveloped in a light so different from ours*
> *that by comparison everything seems dark. When you see*
> *a band of fifty you are lost in amazement. They seem clothed*
> *with golden plates, constantly moving, like so many*
> *suns."*
>
> —Père Lamy

And when Pope Gregory the Great first saw light-skinned English slave boys in a Roman market, he declared that they must be "non angli sed angeli," "not Angles but Angels."

THE SYMBOLOGY OF ANGELS IN ART

"Very early in the history of Art a system of religious symbolism existed, a knowledge of which greatly enhances the pleasure derived from representations of sacred subjects. In no case was this symbolism more carefully observed than in the representations of angels."

—*Clara Erskine Waters*

There are several distinct symbols that came to represent angels in art—wings, halo, flowing robes or draperies, and objects held in the hand like an orb, a scroll, a weapon, a balancing scales, a traveler's walking staff, or an olive branch of peace.

WINGS

"The function of the wing is to take what is heavy and raise it up into the region above, where the gods dwell; of all things connected with the body, it has the greatest affinity with the divine."

—*Plato*

Wings are the most distinctive physical characteristic seen in pictures of angels. They demonstrate spirit, power, and swiftness. That wings lift angels high into the sky suggests great freedom, the angels' transcendence over the suffering of those bound to the earth, and a broad and compassionately understanding view of the affairs of humankind.

The wings of angelic beings are specifically mentioned several times in biblical scripture—in the Old Testament books of Exodus, Isaiah, Ezekiel, Daniel, and Zechariah.

In *Paradise Lost,* John Milton describes the six wings of Raphael:

"A Seraph winged. Six wings he wore, to shade
His lineaments divine; the pair that clad
Each shoulder broad, came mantling o'er his breast
With regal ornament; the middle pair
Girt like a starry zone his waist, and round
Skirted his loins and thighs with downy gold
And colours dipped in Heaven; the third his feet
Shadowed from either heel with feathered mail,
Sky-tinctured grain."

❉

And in his work *Comus,* Milton describes the angels in flight:

"How sweetly did they float upon the wings
Of silence through the empty-vaulted night,
At every fall smoothing the raven down
Of darkness till it smiled!"

❉

As mentioned, one of the earliest-known images of a winged angel was discovered at Ur. Another historically significant work was found on a Jewish-Sumerian carving from the ninth century B.C.—a human face with long hair set on a lion's body, large wings stretching up from its back. Representations of angels with wings were not seen in Christian art until the beginning of the fourth century A.D., in Constantinople. These first Christian images were modeled on Greek figures of the winged goddess Nike, or Victory, but they were portrayed as genderless.

"Come and see. When the sun sets the cherubim . . .
beat their wings above and stretch them out, and the

melodious sound of their wings is heard in the
realms above."
—*The* Zohar, *the "Book of Splendor" of the Cabala*

HALO

The halo—or aureole, or nimbus—is an emanation of golden light around the head, or a bright circle above it, connoting sanctity and spiritual effulgence. Within the aura of the halo the head is sometimes crowned with a royal diadem or tiara to express sovereignty.

Other symbols

The flowing robes or draperies worn by angels in art are usually white to show their purity, but sometimes colors are used. In early Christian art, certain colors were associated with each of the orders of angels—blue with the seraphim, red with the cherubim, etc.

Many times angels hold emblematic objects in their hands—an orb or wand-like scepter showing power and authority, an olive branch showing peace, instruments like a harp or lute showing celebration and harmony, a scroll or codex showing knowledge, and the swords and shields of the militant angels to show faith and righteousness.

As mentioned, certain angels can be identified by their own symbols—Michael by the sword, or by scales; Gabriel by the lily; Raphael by the pilgrim's staff; Uriel by a codex or book.

THE ANGELIC IMAGE TODAY

The idea and vision of angels is very much alive in the hearts and minds of all kinds of people in the world today. In an ever-growing variety of interpretations, the image of the angel continues to be popularly expressed in commercial, spiritual, and secular art.

6 The spirits of our times
Contemporary beliefs and stories of angels

"If you believe there are angels, believe there are angels; and if you don't, don't. But don't tame them into something to which you can be indifferent."
—Ona

p to this point we have only discussed the ideas and experiences that people from the past have had of angels. But what about people today? Do we think about angels? Do we believe in them? Do angels have a personal effect on our lives?

Emphatically, *yes.* Today there is a growing resurgence of the deeply rooted fascination with angels. A recent Associated Press article carried the headline, "An Age for Angels—Spiritual, Commercial Interest in Heavenly Beings on the Rise." The article notes, "Angels are turning up in people's lives with increasing frequency, and people are more receptive to the heavenly beings than ever before. . . . There is widespread belief in angels. Gallup polls have found that half of the nation, including nearly three-

quarters of teenagers, believe in the heavenly beings." The article goes on to document the rapid growth of angel-related organizations and businesses. Even *The Wall Street Journal* acknowledged this rebirth in the prominence of angels, saying, "They are popular with people, religious and otherwise . . . angels are making a comeback . . . riding a crest of interest that crosses denominational lines, linking groups as disparate as Catholics and New Agers, the devout and the unchurched."

A Gallup Youth Survey conducted in September and October of 1992 found that 76 percent of American teenagers ages 13 to 17 believe in angels. This figure is up from 64 percent in 1978 during a period when teen belief in other supernatural and paranormal phenomena has declined.

National groups with local chapters like the Angel Collector's Club gather together to share in their appreciation of angels. Numerous books, workshops, and lecturers help to accommodate the swelling popularity of angels. Across a broad social spectrum there is an expanding sense of wonder attached to angels.

ANGELS IN CONTEMPORARY RELIGIOUS THOUGHT

Though angels are often associated with religious thought, most contemporary western religious institutions do not have anything to say about them in the canons and tenets of their creeds. Though individual thinkers within the Christian Protestant denominations and the Judaic faith have written of angels, these organizations themselves take no official stand about the existence of angels or their place in the spiritual lives of men and women today. The angels' place within these faiths is left to the discretion of individual clerics and to the personal convictions of individual worshipers. Two religious institutions, though, do propose certain ideas about angels as a part of their written dogma: the Roman Catholic Church and the Islamic Ahmadiyya Movement.

ANGELS IN THE ROMAN CATHOLIC CHURCH

The official Church position on angels and their place in Catholic life is stated in *The New Catholic Encyclopedia* and in the annual *Catholic Almanac*. *The New Catholic Encyclopedia* says:

> *"The Church has defined as dogma that besides the visible world, God also created a kingdom of invisible spirits, called angels, and that He created them before the creation of the world. In conformity with Holy Scripture and with the whole Christian tradition, these angels must be regarded as personal beings and not as mere powers or the like . . .*
>
> *"The believing Christian . . . will even today maintain that there are angels because the Bible and the Church teach it . . . He also believes that the angels, inasmuch as they are pure spirits, can never appear in a real body, that as spiritual beings they act on earth in a manner that is unknown to men but verified in Scripture and in the experience of the Christian life of grace . . .*
>
> *"Moreover, in evaluating the accounts taken from the Bible and from Christian tradition, two extremes are to be avoided: on the one hand not everything that is therein contained can be taken as fact, because much of it belongs simply to the philosophy of life in antiquity and must be discarded; so, too, the existence and efficacy of angels cannot be denied out of hand simply because it is possible today, because of more accurate knowledge, to explain by natural causes what was once attributed to angels . . . In this way theology has now come to a point of distinguishing exactly among angels, stars, and the*

powers of nature, and specifies that the nature of angels is completely spiritual and no longer merely a very fine material, firelike and vaporous.

"Up to now it has not yet been defined as dogma that every man has a guardian angel. This opinion does, however, have a basis in Holy Scripture and has been maintained in the Church since ancient times, despite the uncertainty of the question in the first 1,000 years.

"The Church has never declared itself on whether the angels are divided into orders, nor has it said what kinds of orders there might be. Still, it can be drawn from the New Testament that angels exist and are effective in various ways, as can be detected within certain limits. Many questions, however, that are raised in Scripture and tradition relating to the angels cannot be answered or, at least, cannot be answered convincingly, because the necessarily certain knowledge is not possible ... one must be aware that the profane sciences can never prove either the existence or the activity of angels. One knows that angels exist, as St. Augustine once said, through faith."

❋

The glossary of the *Catholic Almanac* describes angels as:

"Purely spiritual beings with intelligence and free will, whose name indicates their mission as ministers of God and ministering spirits to men. They were created before the creation of the visible universe; the devil and bad angels, who were created good, fell from glory through their own fault.

"In addition to these essentials of defined doctrine, it is held that angels are personal beings; they can intercede for persons; fallen angels were banished from God's glory in heaven to hell, bad angels can tempt persons to commit

*sin. The doctrine of guardian angels, although not
explicitly defined as a matter of faith, is rooted in long-
standing tradition. No authoritative declaration has ever
been issued regarding choirs or various categories of angels:
according to theorists, there are nine choirs, consisting of
seraphim, cherubim, thrones, dominations, principalities,
powers, virtues, archangels and angels. In line with
scriptural usage, only three angels can be named—Michael,
Raphael and Gabriel."*

❖

A recent article from the Catholic News Service titled
"Vatican Takes Heavenly Host Seriously" emphasized the
official Catholic belief in angels. Mention was made of a
series of talks given by Pope John Paul II on the subject of
angels, in which he emphasized that "they do exist" and
"have a fundamental role to play in the unfolding of human
events." The article also quoted from a sermon given by
Cardinal Angelo Sodano, Vatican secretary of state, on the
occasion of the Feast of the Guardian Angels: "We thank
the Lord for having placed guardian angels beside us. . . .
The dogma of the existence of angels introduces us to the
wonders worked by God." The Vatican newspaper printed
the entire text of the sermon under the headline: "Guardian
Angels Guide Us and Cheer Us on the Path of Life."

ANGELS IN MODERN ISLAM

Mirza Ghulam Ahmad, the nineteenth-century founder
of the Ahmadiyya Movement in Islam, wrote about core
beliefs of the Moslem faith that were collected in the book
The Essence of Islam, today considered a body of doctrine for
this branch of Islam. Included in this work is a chapter on
the subject of angels. It discusses in a general way the need
for angels in creation, some of their characteristics and

purposes, and the way angels effect the operation of the physical universe and the personal lives of humans:

"The Wisdom of God . . . demanded that . . . there should be a form of creation which should not be veiled by self . . . and should serve God Almighty as His limbs . . . That external creation should possess a nature like transparent mirrors and should be ever present before God Almighty. It should have two directions. One direction should be that of uniqueness and transcendence and, being imperceptible and free from veils, it should be different from the other forms of creation and should resemble completely by ways of reflection the Being of God Almighty . . . The other direction should be that of being created, on account of which they should have a relationship with the rest of creation and should be able to approach them. Thus, through this design of God Almighty, this strange form of creation came into being which is called angels . . .

"They are a species of creation which have independent existence . . . The existence of angels is part of faith . . . We cannot describe their condition in the terms of the conditions of man . . . Allah has described them as standing, in prostration, arranged in rows, glorifying God and occupying their appointed places . . . Angels do not move an inch from the places appointed for them by God Almighty . . .

"Angels do not all have the same status and rank and do not all perform the same kind of functions . . . The function of the angels cannot be without purpose . . . They do not act in vain, but cause various types of movements in heaven and earth in an altogether wise way for the achievement of grand purposes . . .

"It has been established by the Quranic text that the regulators and distributors of all matters from the heaven

*to the earth are angels ... all arrangements that are
carried out between heaven and earth are carried out
through angels ...*

*"The angels carry out the arrangements of the universe,
that is to say, that though on the surface, stars and
the sun and the moon and the elements carry out their
functions, yet in reality it is carried out by angels ... whatever
is happening in the physical system does not take place without
the mediation of angels ...*

*"Those who possess insight behold angels with their
spiritual eyes which they experience very often in a state
of wakefulness. They talk to the angels and learn many
things from them ... The suggestion and revelation that
the angels communicate are according to the nature of
the person concerned ... Every person receives grace
from the suggestion of the angels according to his capacity."*

✿

ANGELS IN THEIR LIVES

Though it is interesting to note that the Catholic Church
and Islam acknowledge angels and attempt to delineate
their relationships with God, the physical universe, and humankind, we have seen how individual each man's and
woman's perceptions and experiences of angels can be.
Each person is touched by angels in a different manner and
has a relationship with them according to their own belief
and choosing.

The stories of three people, in their own words, for
whom the angels play a significant role, are given below.

MARILYNN

Marilynn Webber is a cheerful, outgoing woman with a
very welcoming and accepting manner. A wife and mother
of two grown children, Marilynn's home in Riverside, Cal-

ifornia, houses her personal collection of more than two thousand figures of angels, and her shop and mail-order business, Marilynn's Angels, which sells angel-related gifts and books.

Marilynn's story of being saved by a guardian angel as a teenager in suburban Chicago was included in an October 1992 article in the *Ladies' Home Journal.* Marilynn's own article about her friend Estela, who survived and recovered from an automobile accident with the help of angels, was published in the December 1992 issue of *Guideposts* magazine. Readers responded to this article by sending Marilynn more than 6,000 letters.

Since her college years as a speech major, Marilynn has been a popular lecturer on angels. Twice a week, she hosts "angels teas" at her house, which draw together widely varied groups to talk about their ideas and experiences of angels. The teas have been featured in articles by the *San Francisco Chronicle* and the *Orange County Register* and are booked for months in advance.

"My belief in angels is definitely based on the Bible— that's where I get my basic beliefs of angels. But I have met enough people—and enough people have shared their stories with me—that I know they are very much in evidence today and certainly are helping people not only as guardian angels but as comforting angels, and in many other ways.

"People think of angels mostly as guardian angels, and in many instances, of course, that is true. But in my story of Estela, you will see that this angel did not save her from a terrible accident but her life was spared, and she was given the strength and the courage to face the pain and hardship of the experience.

"That's not new. When you go to the Bible, you'll find

instances like that as well—of angels as comforters and encouragers. So a lot of people say, 'Well, how come the angel didn't save that person from what they went through?' But many times it has been the angels' position to lift people up and to help them through these situations. In this accident, my friend Estela's leg was severed below the knee, and now she has a walker and a prosthesis. But she has risen so far above her disability that she's become an example to people because of the way she feels that this experience has enriched and enhanced her life.

"I received so many letters after the *Guideposts* article—people saying things to me like, 'My little baby was killed in a car crash and it was hard to bear. I was not even with the child at the time. When I read your article I knew that the angels were there and carried the child to heaven.' The article has been a source of encouragement for people, and that is something I think is important.

"My own rescue by an angel was back in the forties. My family was living in Chicago, and my parents decided to move out to a suburb—Wheaton, Illinois. I was in my freshman year at Austin High School in Chicago. I wanted to finish out the year with my friends, so I stayed in the city with friends during the week and went to school. Then on the weekend I would take the Northwestern train to my parents' new home in Wheaton.

"Just before I left to go home one Friday afternoon, I had gotten some very serious news about a friend, who had been my Sunday school teacher. She was someone I looked up to a lot—a very beautiful young woman. I found out she had cancer, and that it was in such an advanced stage she wouldn't live long. I was very disturbed by this, and wondered how such a terrible thing could happen to such a good person. All the way home on the train I was thinking about the unfairness of her life ending so soon when she had been such a wonderful influence to so many people.

"I was preoccupied with this as I got off the train at College Avenue, from where I could walk home. As a matter of habit I got off the train and stood and waited for the train to go on past me. I walked across that track and across another set of tracks with my head down and in a deep depression about my friend. Finally I came to the last set of tracks and was in the middle of them when I became aware of a very loud noise and looked up to see that an approaching train was almost upon me.

"You know, they talk about someone being frozen with fear, and that's exactly what happened to me. I was standing on the tracks, watching the train come, trying to move my legs to get off and not being able to even lift my foot to take a step.

"And so, as I looked up at the train coming, it suddenly came to me that I was going to die. I had a deep faith, and in that moment I believed that I would be in heaven to greet this wonderful teacher of mine that I loved so dearly. In just seconds all this went through my mind, and I was really resigned to die.

"Just before the train hit me I was shoved by a strong force right off the track and down the embankment, where there were a lot of cinders—scratching my hands and my knees. I was so amazed that I had survived, because I had truly expected to be dead in the next moment.

"I was so excited about climbing back up the embankment now that the train had passed by, to see who it was who had saved my life, and to thank them from the bottom of my heart. I hurried back up the tracks, but there was no one there. There was no one even within sight. I had this deep feeling that God had saved my life, and a great warmth and joy came over me.

"When I walked home I shared the experience with my mother. Fortunately she was very wise and believed my story. She told me, 'Yes, I know, that very well could have been an angel that saved you.' So she was a great encouragement. And she said, 'Now that you have been given your life back again, God wants you to count for others in many ways.' And I felt that was a special gift that had been given to me, and I needed to use my life to help other people.

"To this day, I know God was with me in this amazing way, and I feel it was an angel who saved my life. Absolutely, my life was saved—without a doubt and without any question—no one else was there to help. It had to be God's angel. It was a life-changing experience for me, and I will never again be the same.

"My interest in collecting angels goes back to the time I was a child and feared going to bed at night. My mother gave me a beautiful angel figurine to put on my dresser, and told me about Psalm 91:11: 'For he will give his angels charge over you to guard you in all your ways.' Even though it was a very common angel figure by today's standards, to me, it was the most beautiful thing I had ever seen. That angel was my prized possession all through my childhood, and something concrete that reminded me of God's provision of angels in my life.

"Every time I went shopping—which to me in those days was the five-and-dime store—I would ask for angels. And they'd always tell me the same thing: 'Little girl, you'll have to come back at Christmas time, and then we'll have angels.' And, of course, I couldn't wait to save up my money and then find some angels at Christmas time to add to that collection. I was fascinated by angels.

"As people learned of my collection, whenever they would travel or go someplace, they would say, 'What can we bring Marilynn back? Well, you know she collects angels, so we'll just add to her collection.' I still have many of those gifts that hold beautiful memories of the people who gave them to me. That's what makes them so very precious, because so many of them have a beautiful story.

"As my collection grew, and because I was a speech major in college, I was often asked by different groups to come and speak on angels. People would say, 'Why don't ministers preach on angels? They're mentioned at Christmas, and we sing "Hark, the Herald Angels Sing," and that's it. If they're supposed to minister to us daily, why is it we never hear about them?' My talk became very popular, and I would go from church group to women's club to service group to lodges, speaking on angels. People would pass on the word about my lecture. Now I speak all year round, but especially at Christmas time—November and December—and in the spring.

"It is absolutely amazing, the explosion of interest in angels recently. I'm still floored sometimes at what has happened. A while ago I began hosting angel teas in my home, and now I'm booked up completely way in advance. People come here and we talk about angels in our lives. It's a beautiful time for sharing. It is amazing how the teas have grown and how people from all different racial backgrounds, different religious and socio-economic backgrounds, have been involved. I've actually had to limit the sessions some, otherwise I'd have people here every day.

"My shop and mail-order company, Marilynn's Angels, just evolved. It wasn't anything I actively pursued. Having an angel shop of my own was the last thing on my mind a few years ago, but I couldn't find the angels that I wanted anywhere else. I seem to have filled a need out there."

MORDECAI

Mordecai Finley is a rabbi at the Stephen S. Wise Temple, a Jewish Reform congregation in Bel Air, California. He's a big, energetic man with a striking head of red hair and a full red beard. One-sixteenth Irish by blood, Rabbi Finley could pass for a Catholic priest, and is sometimes called "the Irish rabbi" in gentle jest. Mordecai has a bright, intelligent face that looks younger than his thirty-eight years. When he talks it is apparent that his mind moves quickly and clearly, and his enthusiasm for ideas rushes out in a vitality of speech.

Rabbi Finley shares his thoughts about the place of angels within the Judaic faith today, and in his own personal and spiritual life:

"Within the Jewish faith today there is no central authority with the power to issue any kind of official position about the existence of angels and their relationships to God and humankind. It's not a matter of canon. So if you're trying to ascertain contemporary Jewish belief in angels, what you need to do is get an impression of what committed Jews believe.

"The fact that it's not a matter of canon means that it's up to the discretion of each individual rabbi either to say that the parts of the Bible or canon that talk about angels are projections of inner states, or that these [angels] are really emissaries of God that have substantive reality aside from just psychology.

"Typically, the more rationally oriented rabbis—and this is especially from the Reform and Conservative community—express a sense of disbelief in angels as existing beings. Among the more spiritually and mystically oriented rabbis, however, there is an understanding of another dimension of reality—that the worlds connecting the divine realm with the human realm are highly charged, highly in-habited, and animated by various kinds of divine beings, and that's what we mean by angels. And as I work more and more on my own mystical path, my belief in angels grows.

"The Hebrew word for angel, 'malakh,' comes from 'malakha,' which means 'toil,' or 'work.' And a malakh, an angel, really means an agent of God, a worker for God, an emissary of God, as it were, or a messenger. An angel does not necessarily have one form or another. Often in the Bible they appear in regular human form, and it takes a discerning eye to realize an angel is present. In other parts of the Bible—for example, an angel speaks to Abraham, an angel leads the Israelites, an angel speaks to Moses—the angels seem to appear as some kind of mediated energy of God. That would be the best way to describe them. So in the Jewish tradition the angel is not a cherub, or a fat little benign baby. That's just not part of the Jewish—at least biblical and rabbinical—experience of what a malakh is. Rather, the angel can take any shape, any form; it's doing God's work."

"Jewish, rabbinic mythology in midrash [a commentary or exposition on a traditional Hebrew scripture] makes profound use of angels. There's a wonderful midrash on the death of Moses where God sends the angel of death to go down and take Moses' soul. But Moses is too holy, and when the angel of death tries to take his soul, Moses beats him up. The angel goes back to God and says, 'I can't take his soul.' And God says something like, 'I sent you down to do a tough job. You want me to get someone else to take care of it, or are you going to do it?' So there's this great battle between Moses and the angel of death, and Moses tries to enlist the aid of the other angels—the archangels and so forth. It's a wonderful, cosmic story about Moses saying, 'I just want to see the Promised Land. I don't deserve to die, it's not time for me yet.' But God insists that Moses must give up the ghost. It turns out to be a long story, which is beautiful and heart-wrenching.

"The protagonists in this midrash are angels. What did the rabbis think who were writing this story? Were they using angels as props to express their poetic points? Did they believe that there really were angels who fought these kinds of battles and went down and took people's souls? Did they have some kind of primary access to that drama through their knowledge of God? It's hard for me to know. But the ancient rabbis definitely were not ashamed to talk about angels in very direct ways. They were very comfortable with them.

"My experience in Judaism has been what I would call the standard rationalist one, meaning I was never taught specifically about angels in Hebrew school or confirmation. Nor was I taught not to believe in angels. When I studied scripture and saw, for example, that an angel spoke to Abraham, telling him not to go on with the sacrifice of Isaac, it never occurred to me to ask, 'Rabbi, are there really angels?' I just don't think I took the notion seriously enough to even ask the question. I was not dogmatic one way or the other, nor was it presented to me as dogma.

"Early in my life—when I was sixteen or seventeen years old—I began feeling a strong sense of different dimensions of reality, and I knew other people who shared my feelings and taught on the subject. And I met a teacher. He must have been in his forties at that time—a fine man with a very deep soul, who took me on as a kind of a student. It was he who taught me about other levels of reality. And I would say that I became enlightened, or aware, that reality is multi-dimensional, and there are many types or levels of energy permeating existence. That was when I was sixteen, seventeen years old.

"And I would say up until I was in my mid-twenties I

continued to have strong senses of what Jung would call synchronicity, and of having a sense of prescience with myself or other people. I read literature about these things that deeply impressed me—mystical literature, both medieval and modern. It was in the Jewish tradition from many of the Jewish mystical teachers. I would read them secondhand in English because my Hebrew wasn't good enough yet. At that time I never thought much about angels in particular, but in retrospect the work that I was discovering and being introduced to was definitely not against the idea of the existence of angels.

"One of my first great moments in thinking about angels—and this is a story I have often told—was when I was a student rabbi. I used to fly up to Boise, Idaho, from Los Angeles once a month to teach. And in my first few months there I offered to teach an early-morning class on the prayerbook. In teaching different parts of the prayerbook we came soon to the idea of angels. One of the people in the class said, 'What do you think about angels?' And I explained that they are projections of inner psychological processes. And the student said to me, 'So they're in your mind?' And I said, 'Yes.'

"Now there was a woman in the class—a woman who, I found out later, was quite a distinguished poet, an intellectual, and a very deep spiritual person. She attended the class with her husband, who himself was a very profound man—he has a Ph.D. in folklore. But of course I didn't know this. Up in Boise, Idaho, I didn't imagine—my own prejudice—that this depth of knowledge would show up early on a Sunday morning among six other people in the social hall of the synagogue to study the prayerbook.

"So this woman—her name was Ona—raised her hand and said, 'Where in your mind?' So I said, 'What do you mean?' And she said, 'Well, you said angels are in your mind. Do you mean like in your head?' And I said, 'Yes.' And she said, 'Well, where in your head?' So I said, 'They don't have space.' So then she said, 'Then why do you give them a location?' I said, 'That's an excellent point. So what are you getting at?' This is more than ten years ago, but she said something like, 'Saying that angels are in your head or in your mind is taming them into a kind of existence that you don't have to consider. If there are angels, and they don't necessarily take up space, then they're not in your head or outside your head. If you believe there are angels, believe there are angels; and if you don't, don't. But don't tame them into something to which you can be indifferent.' And I immediately said, 'You're right, you're absolutely right. That's exactly what I've done.' And I said, 'I'll have to think about it.' She really challenged me.

"So I went back to Los Angeles, and at the time I had a spiritual teacher there, from the Hassidic tradition. I asked him, 'What are angels to you?' And he said, 'Discreet packets of divine energy doing God's work.' And we talked about the idea that divine energy is mediated, and it becomes manifest in different ways. Perhaps it can even take over a person, causing that person to act for the divine in a given moment. Perhaps that person can be called a 'malakh'—it's better in Hebrew because it doesn't have that baggage that the word 'angel' carries with it in English.

"I haven't had what I would call strong experiences of angels—meaning an angel appearing to me, an angel speaking to me, or something like that. Although there is one incident that I think has a kind of angel sense to it.

"There was a time when I was in Israel, jogging down a road, and an orthodox Jew motioned me over. He tried to convert me to orthodoxy, and he and his friends put me to several tests, informally. And each test they posed to me, I turned back on them, overwhelming them with my knowledge. Now this is what I found very interesting: They would pull out a text and say, 'What do you think about this?' I had studied it in depth somewhere and was able to comment easily. So they would say, 'What do you think about this one?' I began to quiz *them* on it more deeply. And because I had thought deeply about the text, I would ask them questions they couldn't answer to teach them a little lesson. Then they would bring out a harder text— which I had also studied—and then a harder text—which I had also studied—to the point that they were simply overwhelmed by me. They were muttering among themselves, and one of them said, 'You know, with your red hair and your physique, you could be King David. You could be the Messiah.' I playfully said back to him, 'Maybe so,' and I ran off down the road.

"I found out later, back at my kibbutz, that they had come looking for me that night, because I had told them that's where I was staying. Now the person who was in charge of checking in visitors like me was not there when I returned, so he didn't know that I was there. So when the Orthodox Jews came and asked, 'Where's the red-headed guy who's staying here?' he said, 'I've never heard of him, we've never seen such a person.'

"I told this story to another person, and she said to me, 'Mordecai, it just proves the rule that the only thing better than being Elijah is meeting Elijah.' So Elijah is like an angelic figure—meaning an emissary of God who visits people, who enlightens them. So while I didn't view myself as being angelic at that moment, or a messenger of God, I do think that I must have had some profound effect on the mythology of this group. And that experience really made me think about angels. You know, maybe we are unwittingly brought into angelhood, and we do God's work for reasons that we're not even aware of.

"When I was in rabbinical school one day I told my angel story to a good friend of mine and he became quite worried for me. And he said, 'Finley, there aren't angels. Come on, don't go off the deep end here.' And I said, 'What if there might be angels?' He says, 'There aren't angels.' And I said, 'I'll tell you what. Let's flip a coin. If it's heads, I'm committed to believing in angels for the rest of my life. If it's tails, you're committed to believing in angels for the rest of your life. And we'll find out in the next world who was right.' He said, 'Okay,' I think as a way of saving me. So we flipped the coin, and it came out heads. And from that moment I've been committed to a belief in angels. Now whenever I tell this story, at the end I say, 'Clearly, some angel tipped the coin so it came down heads.' (He laughs.)

"So since that time I've playfully read about angels, thought about angels, and so forth. And because now I have an excuse in the form of a solemn promise to my rabbinical school classmate, I believe in a world inhabited by aspects of God's being that mediate God's being to this earthly existence.

"Certainly among the modern world, most rabbis—especially the Conservative and Reform—tend toward rationality and they focus on pragmatism and ethics, which is a focus of mine too. But I have this other strong sense of the angelic world as well. When I tell my angel story, people are delighted, fascinated, moved by it—and they seem to open. I've told them an enchanting first-person story that they find wondrous. I don't think I've changed their dogma, but I might have opened their soul to a different kind of poetry, a different kind of discourse."

JANE

Jane Howard lives in the rural community of Upperco, near Baltimore, Maryland, where she has been employed for nearly two decades at an advertising agency. But Jane feels her real vocation is the ten years she has spent working in her evenings, weekends, and vacations, giving lectures, workshops, and one-on-one "readings" with people seeking to learn more about angels and to form personal, communicative relationships with them. As an angel enthusiast, Jane has traveled and lectured worldwide and has appeared on national television. In 1992, her book *Commune with the Angels: A Heavenly Handbook,* was published by the Association for Research and Enlightenment.

Though many of the people questioned and interviewed for this book believe they've had personal contact with angels, Jane is unusual in that she regularly sees and hears angels quite directly. It is apparent within a few seconds of conversation with her that Jane's life has been profoundly touched by her experiences with the angels, and she considers it a joyful service to share her stories and knowledge with others.

"I see angels in many forms. I can see them when they take on the form of a male or a female. I can see them as an energy—like a wave, a rippling effect of different colors of energy when they want to make themselves known that way. Regardless, I do actually see them as clearly as I see human beings. I see them with what I call 'inner eyes'—I know it's beyond my eyes, almost inside of my eyes. To me the angels are as plain and as real as a human being. There've been so many wonderful times, for example, when I've looked over in my car and I've seen my guardian angel actually sitting there in physical form.

"And I hear them as plain as day. I hear them as if I am hearing someone speak.

"Many people say to me, 'Well, how do you know you're communicating with angels?' I believe each and every person is accountable to God as to what we do in our lives. I know in my heart of hearts that I am working with the angelic kingdom because of the joy and the light and the love that they've brought into my life. When people ask me, 'How can you believe in angels?' I cannot *not* believe, because of all the experiences that I've had personally—the many times when they've saved my life, when they've done large-scale things for me. And even more times when they've been there for me daily, to assist and to guide me. Not to run my life, but to give helpful hints, and help me make the connections that will be for my highest good, and lead to the most joyous life experiences.

"From early childhood I have seen angels—around eleven years old. I became aware of the presence of angelic beings in my room. They took on the appearance of a large white canopy of light that enveloped the entire ceiling of my bedroom, watching over me when I went to sleep. At that time there was only an awareness between us. Then as a teenager I really opened up to the angels and became aware that I was hearing them and communicating. I talked back and forth with them pretty much as unseen friends, but I knew they were angels.

"When I was in my late twenties, I started opening up spiritually. I was studying, and doing workshops with numerous healers—I wanted to know anything that was metaphysical. I accumulated a great deal of information on the angels, since that was one thing in particular that I wanted to know more about. I knew they were very much in my life, but no one was talking about them. There was little information out there, and so I started doing research and accumulating files of Dionysius' work and biblical stories and just anything I could get my hands on.

"Then I had an experience where the angels saved my life. I was driving my car and was not aware that wires had shorted underneath the hood that would cause the car to catch on fire. The angels guided me to unload my car before the fire started, and they protected me from harm as I stood back from the burning vehicle. They were like a fortress in front of the car, telling me, 'Everything's going to be all right, Janie, even though it looks pretty scary. It's going to be okay.' And it was.

"The angels are messengers of God, and my service at this time is to act as a messenger for the angels to spread the word about them, mainly so people will know of their availability and their willingness to assist in our lives. My role is to give lectures and workshops about the angelic kingdom, sharing my personal experiences, and using historical references. I work to inspire people to have a close relationship with the angels so that the angels will be able to touch people's lives and inspire them. I help people to realize the beautiful beings that angels are and that they're part of God's plan as a resource available to us as children of God.

"I run workshops worldwide, and I do personal readings for people—one-on-one, or by mail or phone. During that reading I introduce people to their own guardian angel, allowing them to experience the sensation of the presence of the angel and of receiving messages for themselves. I do not in any way want to be a guru, and the angels do not want to be worshipped. They want to foster a friendship and a relationship, so I encourage people, after they've had the session with me, to go on and develop that relationship. The process will be different for each person. I'm simply teaching them to get on the bicycle by providing the training wheels. Hopefully they're going to take off the training wheels themselves and let that relationship fly in whatever way is for their highest good.

"During the session they experience what it's like to

commune with their guardian. The angels are always there; they're always in our energy fields. We just choose whether or not to be conscious of them. When I work with people they are ready to take that leap of faith where their experience moves from the unconscious into the consciousness.

"I have found that people have a foundation for a relationship with angels in their subconscious—in some way they have already been exposed to the idea of angels. And whether or not they've had a conscious personal experience, they do believe. They believe in the angels on the Christmas cards, they believe in the angels in the biblical stories. So it's a transformational experience when they bring all that into their own conscious reality.

"Angels are a reflection of goodness, of wholeness. I'd say one reason I encourage people to work with angels is because they know no separation from God. So when we're sad and blue, when we're feeling left out, it's then that the angels give us that wonderful reflection that no matter what we feel we've lost, in fact we really have lost nothing, because we're at one with God.

"My work now is to establish a 'Be an Angel Day'—to be celebrated annually on August 22. In numerology, 22 is known as the master architect number, the master builder. The angels chose the twenty-second because we're trying to build something significant on a large scale. The celebration of this day is a bridge being built between the kingdoms of humankind and the angels. August was chosen partly for the simple reason that there is no other major holiday in August. August is also the eighth month. In numerology, the number eight is a prosperity symbol of fulfillment, achievement, and success. The angels chose the eighth month because we're going to be achieving something on a master level.

The motto for the day is 'Be an Angel'—do one small act

of service for someone, be a blessing in someone's life. According to the angels, it is now time to establish an outward cooperation between the kingdoms—between the human kingdom and the angelic kingdom—so that people will see that they can be earth angels. If there's one word that describes the angels, it's 'service.' We too can be angels in other people's lives by doing a small act of service, simply by reaching out to someone."

AN OPEN INVITATION

The author, David Connolly, is publisher of the bi-monthly newsletter *AngelShare*, a forum for learning and sharing about angels, and he invites your thoughts and experiences. If you would like to contact Mr. Connolly, or wish to subscribe to the newsletter, write to:

AngelShare
P.O. Box 41454
Santa Barbara, CA 93140-1454

Glossary of Angelic Terms

Angelolatry: The veneration or worship of angels.

Angelology: The study of angels.

Angelophany: An angel visitation.

Angelos: Greek translation of the Hebrew word "malakh," for messenger, from which the English word "angel," is derived.

Archangel: Classification of angel thought to be higher than ordinary angels. In the system of the angelic hierarchy given by Pseudo-Dionysius, archangels are one of the nine orders of angels. In traditional Judaic and Christian angelology, there are thought to be seven archangels.

Aureole: (See "Halo")

Cherubim: One of the orders of angels in both Judaic and Christian angelology. The cherubim are mentioned and described in the Bible.

Choir: In the organization of angels described by Pseudo-Dionysius, there are orders of angels, each of which is divided into three choirs.

Choristers: Musical angels.

Codex: Scroll of parchment or paper sometimes depicted in the hands of angels in artistic representations to show knowledge and authority.

Diadem: Crownlike ornament covering the head sometimes included in pictures of angels to show sovereignty, power, and authority. (See also "Tiara")

Draperies: Angelic robes.

Fioretti: Occasions of intervention by angels in the affairs of humans.

Halo: Emanation of light around the head of an angel, or a circle of light around the head of an angel, used in artistic representations of angels to show sanctity and spiritual radiance. (See also "Aureole," "Nimbus")

Host: A gathering of angels.

Malakh: Hebrew word for angel meaning "emissary" or "messenger."

Manna: A kind of heavenly bread mentioned in the Old Testament that is said to be the food of the angels.

Nimbus: (See "Halo")

Order: One of several levels or groups of angels in the organization of all the angels as a whole. For example, in the celestial hierarchy described by Pseudo-Dionysius, there are nine orders of angels.

Orb: A small globe, often golden and surmounted by a cross, sometimes held in the hand of angels in art to represent sovereignty and heavenly authority.

Putti: Fat, winged babies sometimes representing angels in art, which are also referred to as cherubs (not to be confused with "cherubim," one of the traditional orders of angels in Judaic and Christian belief).

Quodlibet: A theological or philosophical fine point debated by medieval scholars.

Scepter: A rod or wand, often golden in color, sometimes shown in the hands of angels in art to demonstrate their sovereignty and heavenly authority.

Seraphim: One of the orders of angels in Judaic and Christian angelology.

Throne Angels: The four angels thought to stand one to each side of the throne of God in heaven—usually said to be Michael, Gabriel, Raphael, and Uriel.

Tiara: (See "Diadem")

Bibliography

Adler, Mortimer Jerome. *The Angels and Us*. New York: Macmillan, 1982.

Ahmad, Mirza Ghulam. *Essence of Islam*. Translated by Muhammad Zafrullah Khan. London: Alden Press, 1981.

Apocrypha, The. Translated by Edgar J. Goodspeed. Chicago: University of Chicago Press, 1938.

Augustine, St. *City of God*. Translated and edited by Marcus Dods. New York: Hafner Publishing Company, 1948.

Bible, The Holy. Revised Standard Version. New York: Thomas Nelson & Sons, 1952.

Blake, William. *The Complete Prose and Poetry of William Blake*. Edited by David V. Erdman. Garden City, New York: Anchor Books, 1982.

Book of Enoch, The. Edited by R. H. Charles. Oxford: Clarendon Press, 1893.

Book of Tobit, The. Edited by A. D. Neubauer. Oxford: Clarendon Press, 1878.

Brewer, E. Cobham. *A Dictionary of Miracles.* Philadelphia: J. B. Lippincott Company, 1884.

Buber, Martin. *Tales of Angels, Spirits and Demons.* Translated by David Antin and Jerome Lothberg. New York: Hawk Wells Press, 1938.

Calvin, John. *Institutes of the Christian Religion.* Vol. I, Book I. Translated by John Allen. Philadelphia: Philip H. Nicklin, 1816.

Cameron, Ann. *The Angel Book.* New York: Ballantine Books, 1977.

Catholic Almanac. Edited by Felican Foy. Huntington, Indiana: Our Sunday Visitor, Inc., 1992.

Clement, Clara Erskine. *Angels in Art.* Boston: L. C. Page & Co., 1898.

Crockett, Silvia. *Angels in Traditional Design.* Owings Mills, Maryland: Stemmer House Publishers, 1987.

Davidson, Gustav. *A Dictionary of Angels.* New York: The Free Press, 1967.

Eddy, Mary Baker. *Science and Health.* Boston: Trustees of the Will of Mary Baker G. Eddy, 1934.

Dante Alighieri. *The Divine Comedy.* Translated by Henry Francis Clay. New York: Oxford University Press, 1950.

Dickinson, Emily. *The Complete Poems of Emily Dickinson.* Boston: Little, Brown, 1924.

Encyclopaedia Biblica. Edited by T. K. Cheyne and J. Sutherland Black. New York: The Macmillan Company, 1899.

Encyclopaedia Judaica. Edited by Geoffrey Wigoder. Jerusalem: The Macmillan Company, 1972.

Encyclopedia of Religion, The. Edited by Mircea Eliada. New York: Macmillan, 1987.

Ginzberg, Louis. *The Legends of the Jews.* Translated by Henrietta Szold. Philadelphia: The Jewish Publication Society of America, 1909.

Graham, Billy. *Angels: God's Secret Agents.* Garden City, New York: Doubleday, 1975.

Hahn, Emily. *Breath of God.* Garden City, New York: Doubleday, 1971.

Heywood, Thomas. *The Hierarchie of the Blessed Angells*. London: Adam Islip, 1635.

Hobbes, Thomas. *Leviathan; or the Matter, Forme and Power of a Commonwealth, Eclesiasticall and Civil*. Edited by Michael Oakeslott. Oxford: Blackwell, n.d.

Howard, Jane M. *Commune with the Angels: A Heavenly Handbook*. Virginia Beach, Virginia: A.R.E. Press, 1992.

Jewish Encyclopedia, The. Edited by Isidore Singer. New York: Funk and Wagnalls, 1912.

Koran. Translated by N.J. Dawood. New York: Penguin Books, 1990.

Longfellow, Henry Wadsworth. *The Poetical Works of Longfellow*. Boston: Houghton Mifflin, 1975.

Maimonides, Moses. *The Guide of the Perplexed*. Translated by Shlomo Pines. Chicago: University of Chicago Press, 1963.

Man, Myth and Magic: An Illustrated Encyclopedia of the Supernatural. Edited by Richard Cavendish. New York: Marshall Cavendish Corporation, 1970.

Milton, John. *Paradise Lost*. New York: The Heritage Press, 1940.

———. *The Poems of John Milton*. Edited by F. W. Bateson. New York: W. W. Norton, 1968.

New Catholic Encyclopedia. Edited by William J. McDonald. New York: McGraw-Hill, 1967.

New Jerusalem Bible, The. Edited by Henry Wansbrough. Garden City, New York: Doubleday, 1985.

New Jewish Encyclopedia. Edited by David Bridger. New York: Behrman House, 1962.

Newman, John Henry. *A Newman Treasury*. Edited by Charles Frederich Harrold. New York: Longmans, Green, 1943.

Old Testament Pseudepigrapha, The. Edited by James H. Charlesworth. Garden City, New York: Doubleday, 1983.

Oxford Dictionary of Modern Quotations, The. Edited by Tony Augarde. New York: Oxford University Press, 1991.

Oxford University Press Dictionary of Quotations, The. New York: Crescent Books, 1985.

Poe, Edgar Allan. *The Complete Tales and Poems of Edgar Allan Poe*. New York: Vintage Books, 1975.

Pseudo-Dionysius, the Areopagite. *Celestial Hierarchy*. Translated by John Parker. London: Skeffington, 1894.

———. *Mystical Theologia*. London: Shrine of Wisdom, 1949.

Regamey, R. P. *Anges*. Paris: Pierre Tisne, 1946.

Reynolds, John. *Inquiries Concerning the State and Economy of the Angelic Worlds*. London: John Clark, 1723.

Rilke, Rainer Maria. *Duino Elegies*. Translated by J. B. Leishman and Stephen Spender. New York: W. W. Norton, 1939.

Shakespeare, William. *Hamlet*. Edited by Alan Durband. London: Hutchinson, 1988.

———. *Macbeth*. Edited by G. K. Hunter. London: Penguin Books, 1988.

Swedenborg, Emanuel. *Angelic Wisdom Concerning the Divine Love and Wisdom*. London: Swedenborg Society, 1969.

Thomas Aquinas, Saint. *Summa Contra Gentiles*. Book 3: Providence. Translated by Vernon J. Bourke. Notre Dame, Indiana: University of Notre Dame Press, 1975.

———. *Summa Theologiae*. Vol. 14. Translated by J. C. O'Brian. Great Britain: Blackfriars, 1975.

Tishby, Isaiah. *The Wisdom of the Zohar*. Translated by David Goldstein. New York: Oxford University Press, 1989.

Universal Jewish Encyclopedia, The. Edited by Isaac Landman. New York: Universal Jewish Encyclopedia, 1939.

Von Grunebaum, Gustave E. *Muhammadan Festivals*. New York: Henry Schuman, 1951.

Ward, Theodora. *Men and Angels*. New York: Viking Press, 1969.

Wilson, Peter Lamborn. *Angels*. New York: Pantheon Books, 1980.

Webster's New World Dictionary of Quotable Definitions. Edited by Eugene E. Brussel. Englewood Cliffs, NJ: Prentice Hall, 1988.

Wesley, John. *The Letters of the Rev. John Wesley, A.M.* Edited by John Telford. London: Epworth Press, 1931.

Wolfson, Harry Austrya. *Philo: Foundations of Religious Philosophy in Judaism, Christianity and Islam*. Cambridge, Massachusetts: Harvard University Press, 1948.

Works of Aurelius Augustine, Bishop of Hippo, The. Edited by Marcus Dods. Edinburgh: T. & T. Clark, 1872.

List of Illustrations

Cover: "Israfel," lithograph by Hugo Steiner-Prag (1943), for *The Poems of Edgar Allan Poe*, © 1943 by The Limited Editions Club, Inc. Used by permission of the publisher.

8 Detail from "Angels Descending the Heavenly Ladder," engraving by Gustave Doré (c. 1868) from Dante's *Paradiso* (Canto 21).

12 "Angel Holding a Star," German woodcut (c. 1505) from *Der Beschlossengart des Rosenkrantz Marie.*

21 "Angel Preventing Abraham from Sacrificing Isaac," woodcut (c. 1495), from *Spiel der Menschilcher.* Photo from the collection of the Library of Congress.

28 Detail from "The Annunciation," woodcut by Albrecht Dürer (c. 1502), from *Life of the Virgin.*

31 Detail from "Christ Surrounded by Musical Angels," painting by Hans Memling (c. 1480), Musée d'Art, Auvers. Photo credit: Giraudon/Art Resource, NY. Used by permission.

43 Drawing of Daniel in the lions' den by Silvia Crockett, after

an illustration by Stephanus Garcia (c. 975), from *Beatus Apocalypse.* © 1987 by Silvia S. Crockett.

47   "Battle of Heaven," engraving by Gustave Doré (c. 1866), from Milton's *Paradise Lost.*

53   "The Seven Angels with a Cross and the Six Keys Receive a Soul into Heaven," woodcut by Albrecht Dürer (c. 1488), from *Bruder Klaus.*

56   "The Annunciation," tempera on wood painting by Masolino da Panicale (c. 1425), National Gallery of Art, Washington, D.C., Andrew Mellon Collection. © 1993 by the National Gallery of Art. Used by permission.

63   "The Descent of the Angels to One of the Daughters of Men," graphite drawing on laid paper by William Blake (c. 1824), from the *Book of Enoch,* the National Gallery of Art, Washington, D.C., Rosenwald Collection. © 1993 National Gallery of Art. Used by permission.

74   "The Saintly Throng in the Form of a Rose," engraving by Gustave Doré (c. 1868) from Dante's *Paradiso* (Canto 31).

88   "St. Michael the Archangel," terracotta by Andrea della Robbia (c. 1475), Metropolitan Museum of Art, New York, Harris Brisbane Dick Fund, 1960. All rights reserved, The Metropolitan Museum of Art. Used by permission.

89   "St. Michael Fighting the Dragon," woodcut by Albrecht Dürer (c. 1498), from *The Revelation of St. John.* Photo from the collection of the Library of Congress.

94   Detail of Gabriel, from "Annunciation," painting by Jan and Hubert Van Eyck (c. 1432), Ghent Altarpiece, Cathedrale Saint-Bavone, Ghent. Photo credit: Giraudon/Art Resource, NY. Used by permission.

100   "Angel of Revelation," watercolor with pen and ink by William Blake (c. 1805), The Metropolitan Museum of Art, New York, Rogers Fund, 1914. All rights reserved, The Metropolitan Museum of Art. Used by permission.

108   "The Pillared Angel," woodcut by Albrecht Dürer (c. 1498), from *The Revelation of St. John.*

114   Detail of "Jacob Wrestling the Angel," engraving by Gustave Doré (c. 1866), from the Bible.

118 Drawing of angel with big wings by Silvia Crockett, after a figure from the 15th century French repoussé silver gilt monstrance reliquary at the Church of Rigardase. © 1987 by Silvia S. Crockett.

121 Drawing of angel with scepter by Silvia Crockett, after a design of an 11th century Italian raised gilt copper book cover. © 1987 by Silvia S. Crockett.

124 "Angel," india ink and brush on paper by Marc Chagall (1954), © 1993 ARS, New York/ADAGP, Paris. Used by permission.

126 "The Annunciation," painting by El Greco (c. 1597). The Toledo (Ohio) Museum of Art. Used by permission.